A Space for Silence

ALEN MACWEENEY   CARO NESS

A Space for Silence

FRANCES LINCOLN

For Hazel - A.M.

For Frances Lincoln, who put her trust in me.
For Joan, Graeme, Ginnie, David and Julia, my family, who all watch over me.
For friends, old and new, who challenge and inspire me - C.N.

Frances Lincoln Limited
4 Torriano Mews
Torriano Avenue
London NW5 2RZ

A Space for Silence
Copyright © Frances Lincoln Limited 2002
Original text copyright © Caro Ness 2002
Photographs copyright © Alen MacWeeney 2002

First Frances Lincoln edition: 2002

British Library Cataloguing-in-Publication Data
A catalogue record for this book is available
from the British Library.

ISBN 0 7112 1656 8

Designed by Becky Clarke
Index by Vicky Robinson

Set in The Sans and Chicago

Printed and bound in Singapore

2 4 6 8 9 7 5 3 1

Contents

Foreword

The impulse to carve out a zone at home for prayer or reflection has its roots in ancient cultures, yet it flourishes today with a new vitality. An intimate domestic sanctuary may be a place to worship, to meditate, or simply to be – an oasis of calm amid the myriad distractions of contemporary life. More than that, it may serve as a refuge, a place to come to terms with the pressures and anxieties of an uncertain world.

Seldom in recent memory has the need for a spiritual haven seemed so compelling. It is shared these days not only by religious individuals but also by those not attached to a particular faith. Such havens may have been inspired by a single religion or by a diversity of faiths or non-traditional systems of belief. And while they are often conceived as an individual's conduit to unseen worlds, they are by no means confined to the domestic realm.

In researching this book, the author and photographer visited private homes, communal spaces and public institutions, portions of which were set aside for worship or meditation. In almost

every instance, the unifying force of such spaces was their creator's intention: to give his or her spirituality a place to spread its wings.

In keeping with that purpose, the sanctuaries in this book are often sumptuous, filled with ritual objects and icons, drenched in light and shimmering colour. But just as often, they are as spare as a friar's cell, decorated with little more than an artful arrangement of prayer rugs, pictures and screens.

Generally, such environments are incorporated into their owner's everyday world, their elements fixed and tangible. Such is the case in the home of Alice Harris, a New York City writer, who has given a place of honour in her cherry-wood kitchen to an ancient carved Japanese deity. Her goddess presides, a reassuring and protective presence, over her family dining-table.

In some instances, such spiritual zones migrate, perpetually shifting landscapes. Gurmukh, a Sikh and a teacher of yoga in Los Angeles, likes to move her ever-expanding collection of statues and objects from place to place in her home because, as she explains, 'I like to feel my interactive relationship with God.'

In forging a link between the spiritual and temporal worlds, some of our subjects have created reflecting pools or gardens – the latter regarded in some cultures as a symbol of paradise on earth. For Allison Fonte, a Manhattan rooftop garden certainly fulfils that function. Redolent with exotic shrubs and flowers, it is a place that energizes and restores her, filling her with quiet joy. 'My garden,' she says, is a way of 'making other people see the abundance that I feel inside.'

The intimate sanctuaries in this book foster balance and harmony by speaking to each of the senses. Nor do solid walls invariably define them. Communication with the divine may be cultivated through channels as elusive and impermanent as the scent of flowers or the soothing play of chimes. Few people better understand the evocative power of scent than John Steele, a perfumer in California, who has researched the use of Alaskan flower essences for room sprays designed to transform any part of one's home into a sacred space. Fragrant, rich in sounds, textures and exalted imagery, his home, like each of the intimate havens in this book, suggests that a journey through the senses may well be the swiftest pathway to the soul.

Ruth La Ferla

Introduction

Regardless of race, creed or culture, humanity has sought, since the earliest times, to find a deeper meaning behind life's mysteries and has created gods and goddesses to explain the inexplicable. Whether it is ancient man trying to explore and explain his environment or a Hindu today seeking enlightenment through the Vedas, the intention was ever the same, to be alive to the whole question of what it means to be human.

Despite the commercial and materialistic thrust of our world today, many religions are thriving, even though they may have changed in form and expression since their inception. Religion – or more broadly speaking, faith – remains a vital inspirational force in many people's lives.

And yet, whilst many still worship in a communal environment as they have for millennia, a significant number of people are now searching for peace, solace or inspiration in a private place. This need not preclude attending a formal place of worship, but it does reflect the need that people feel to find a space in their own environment in which, simply, to be. This book reflects that need and describes some inspirational responses to it.

You will notice that each location has been photographed as an empty space. Our hope is that the spaces will speak for themselves and you, the readers, can place yourselves in them. We trust that in some small, yet infinitely profound way, they will touch you as they did us, and open your eyes to the beauty of Spirit.

Urban

Oases

Urban Oases
Spiritual Retreats in the City

We connect to the world through sound: the chatter of people, the hum of traffic, the whisper of touch, the percussion of a heartbeat. Sound is such an integral part of our everyday life that we often overlook it: sound gives us pleasure when listening to beautiful music or birdsong, it helps us to communicate with each other, and it can alert us to impending danger or to a technical problem. Yet, in our increasingly urban world of myriad stimuli, many sounds are unpleasant, annoying or unwelcome; we refer to these as noise.

Noise is now viewed as one of the most pervasive pollutants. Excessive exposure to noise affects health and well-being. It can contribute to the development or aggravation of problems such as hearing loss, high blood pressure, coronary disease, ulcers, colitis, migraine headaches and possibly viral infection. In addition, it can affect our sleep patterns, concentration and therefore productivity. Research has shown that more than 20 million Americans are regularly exposed to industrial or recreational noise that could result in hearing loss and approximately one-third of the 28 million cases of hearing loss reported are partially due to noise pollution.

Research has also shown that a quiet environment helps both adults and children communicate and learn better. For centuries this is something that meditators have understood, for whilst we experience the world through our senses and our actions, meditation allows us to experience the world through inner channels.

In the past, many who sought the tranquillity of meditation chose to do so in seclusion, often in caves and later on, in monasteries and convents. The word 'monastery' is thought to be derived from the Ancient Greek word *mónos* meaning 'alone' or *monasterion* meaning 'to live alone', for originally such places were individual cells within a collective inhabited by hermits and meditators who craved solitude. In the early Christian tradition, hermits or miracle workers who chose a life of contemplation and selfless service to others were honoured as saints, a practice which evolved from the Jewish tradition of honouring holy men and women with shrines.

In our own time, growing numbers of people are discovering for themselves the benefits of meditation. The author Trevor Leggett has written extensively about the effect of practising either meditation or sport. Time and place are important to both disciplines. If a particular exercise is practised at the same time every day, the body becomes used to the routine and the metabolism responds and changes accordingly. It is the same with meditation. If you are accustomed to sitting quietly to meditate at the same time every day, your body starts to anticipate the routine of relaxing and being still. Most people find that meditation is best done early in the morning or last thing at night because their environment is more likely to be peaceful and interruption is less likely.

As the Buddhist author, Richard St Ruth says, 'Buddha means "awakened", so when we start to meditate we are working towards an awakening. However, if we assume, as in Zen, that we are Buddha from the beginning, then it becomes a question of staying in that time or moment so that we can reawaken our Buddhahood. As practitioners become more experienced, they are able to stay in a contemplative state regardless of circumstance or time. This awakeness therefore transcends both physical and mental states. One of the principal teachings of Tibetan Buddhism uses the analogy of a bird flying through space. This is how we should live our lives, by staying in the moment and not leaving tracks.'

A ROOFTOP PARADISE

NEW YORK, USA

Allison Fonte

Allison Fonte, president of Fonte Public Relations, a Soho-based PR firm, says that the irony of living in New York is that everyone loves the pace of the city – and yet they all try to escape it at weekends or in the summer. Allison herself no longer feels that need, for on her roof terrace the din of the world is stilled. As she says, 'It is much simpler to integrate peace into your everyday life than to move.'

When Allison acquired her apartment, the roof terrace consisted of black tar and utilitarian decking, but it catches the sun all day, so she decided to make it an extension of her apartment. She set out to create a space that would transport her to another place and dimension – not to be used for meditation in the traditional sense, but as a place of calm and tranquillity. Gardening is Allison's meditation; she derives extraordinary inner peace and quiet from it. The fact that she is creating something beautiful out of such a simple activity, using her hands to turn the soil, to water the flowers, to tend each plant, is a constant source of wonder to her. 'I can be completely exhausted, at the end of a long day – but when I walk out on to this terrace, it embraces me with a stillness which revives me.'

The garden is a tropical paradise humming with life, vivid with colour, intoxicating the senses. A Sri Lankan datura tree hangs over an arbour at the end of the terrace. The arbour is composed of a beautiful, hand-carved Nuristani mantel and a simple steel structure which supports the birch crossbeams to give shade to anyone sitting below. The mantel contains a magnificent African throne, partly shrouded with fine hemp curtains.

Allison likes to experiment with the shapes of leaves or flowers, the hues of plants, and to feel the impact of new colour or shape in the garden. Constantly evolving, it is a visible manifestation of nature's wealth and bounty. 'I wouldn't call myself a spiritual person, but I have found a connection to beauty in my garden. It is a way of making other people see the abundance that I feel inside.'

RIGHT AND OPPOSITE:
Pierre Sernet's Zen
tea-house and garden
exude the spirit of Zen:
tatami mats, shoji screens
and the simple objects
associated with the tea
ceremony are carefully
arranged in the shelter
and a highly stylized
garden leads to the hut.

A TEA-HOUSE IN MANHATTAN
NEW YORK, USA
Pierre Sernet

The lively exuberance of Allison Fonte's rooftop garden is in complete contrast to the *roji* (tea ceremony) garden and tea-house, built by Pierre Sernet on the roof of a Manhattan town house. His object was to create an inspiring yet peaceful environment that would allow him to leave professional pressures behind. The garden, designed first, is intended to be viewed from the sliding windows of the master bedroom; a space was left to incorporate the tea-house later on.

The garden is a triumph of simplicity, following closely the Zen principle that a sacred space is complete when nothing more can be taken away from it. Yet Pierre Sernet has managed to include eight trees and countless shrubs and bushes within this 42 x 20 foot garden, including a sequoia and a black pine, a branch of which he has trained to fall gracefully by weighting it with a hanging stone.

The roji garden was designed with a group of trees in the middle to trick the eye into believing that it is bigger than it really is. The path's stepping-stones get progressively smaller as you move away from the *engawa* (covered balcony) and towards the tea-house; they then change direction to encourage the visitor to seek out the small stone statues of Buddha or Jizoo Bosatsu that are tucked into the undergrowth. As Pierre Sernet puts it, 'A Japanese garden should look completely natural, although in the creation of it nothing is left to chance.'

When he built the tea-house ten years later, Pierre went to the Urasenke Chanoyu Center in New York to study the art of the tea ceremony, which he performs, on average, once a week during the spring and summer months and once a month in the fall. 'People say that it is a rigorous, structured and complex art, but you learn the ceremony essentially in order to share a bowl of tea! I prepare the room, the flowers, the scroll with attention to the seasons and the particular guest at that time, and the beauty of the ceremony emerges irrespective of the fact that it is a precisely-structured ritual. There comes a time in the process when I can communicate with my guest in a spiritual, emotional and intellectual manner, rather than on a purely physical level. At the end of the day, the tea ceremony is a means of shutting out the world and putting myself in a different dimension – while sharing a bowl of tea.'

THE T SALON
NEW YORK, USA
Miriam Novalle

Miriam Novalle would agree with Pierre Sernet. If you walk away from the chaos and buzz of East 20th Street, between 5th Avenue and Broadway, and into her T Salon, you will encounter a haven of tranquillity devoted to tea. It is as if you have walked out of a tornado into an ocean of calm, in which you feel you want to bathe indefinitely. Above the tea-room is a beautiful meditation room, popular with meditation groups and also used for summer solstice celebrations, for Chi Kung and Feng Shui workshops and for healing therapy.

The whole building exudes a wonderful peace. Miriam feels that this is what tea-drinking is all about and says that during the construction of the T Salon, she and a friend, a Buddhist monk, meditated on the site each morning and placed energy-balancing crystals on the floor. 'In the rush of New York City, people regard this place as their sanctuary. I wanted to create a space where you can sit for hours and quietly be, but the truth is that I didn't create this space – tea did. I'm just the servant: tea is the master, the magician who conjured up this sacred, blissful space. I believe it has a delicate soul. Like a good pair of shoes, it keeps you safe and secure.'

ABOVE: The water container (*mizusashi*), tea container (*chaire*), tea bowl (*chawan*), tea whisk (*chasen*), tea scoop (*chashsku*) and napkin are all vital components of the Japanese tea ceremony. Each of these utensils, known collectively as *chadogu*, has been selected for its aesthetic qualities.

OPPOSITE, RIGHT AND PAGES 14–15: Here, simplicity governs
construction and design, yet nature prevails on ivy-covered
walls and in the retracting roof that allows all kinds of light
to suffuse the pool and the room below it.

A PAVILION IN GREENWICH VILLAGE
NEW YORK, USA
Raymond and Deneen King

The poet Philip Larkin once remarked, 'If I had a religious symbol, it would be water.' This could equally be said of the former home of Raymond and Deneen King. Their two-storey pavilion in Greenwich Village, built around a spacious courtyard and reflecting pool, now houses a thriving fashion empire, untrammelled despite the commercial activity.

Deneen is deeply nostalgic about it. 'There was always something intensely nurturing about that house, which is why I always refer to her in the feminine. At the same time, it had a spiritual quality, which was connected to the reflecting pool. You heard the water before you saw it, and it was moving and invigorating, but on seeing the pool, you stopped, were stilled and replenished.' Deneen likens the response it engendered in her to the feeling of harmony, liberation and utter bliss that you get riding a horse with which you have total empathy.

Constructed on the model of a Roman atrium, the shallow rectangular pool, with its small frog fountains and ivy-covered walls, is lit from above by a glass roof that retracts to let in rain, snow or sunlight according to the seasons. 'Seeing the sunlight in the morning filtering down through the water was always liberating, and the pool's glass bottom suffused the living-room below with a wonderful light. No matter how many times we looked at this room, we got a rush. It was as if we had our own oasis.'

The Kings always meditated by the pool, yet they do not use the word 'meditate', preferring 'reflect' instead. 'You stepped away from conflict, contemplated what was wrong, and reflected on the answer to a particular question,' says Deneen, 'and the reflective pool, the sight of it, the sound of it filling the house, always helped you in that process.'

A YOGA ROOM IN BEVERLY HILLS

CALIFORNIA, USA

Eric Small

Some people living in a busy city carry their sacred space around inside them; or they simply stay where they are, meeting their spiritual needs in their immediate environment. This is true on both counts of Eric Small, the distinguished Iyengar yoga teacher. He is a remarkable man carrying the joy and innocence of the inner child within him – and yet, working as he does to teach and learn universal love, he never feels the need to venture into Los Angeles from his home in Beverly Hills!

When Eric Small confronts a room full of people with multiple sclerosis, he walks into the room, sits cross-legged in a chair and says, 'Hello, my name is Eric Small, I'm an Iyengar yoga teacher, I've had MS for 50 years and I'm going to show you how you can start your life again. It's as simple as that.'

The spiritual path followed by Eric is truly inspirational. Diagnosed with multiple sclerosis at the age of 21, his condition gradually deteriorated. By 1968, only able to walk with a pair of crutches, he decided to take up yoga and attempted to attend a class given by Iyengar at Berkeley. The class was full and Eric was refused entry, despite his circumstances, so he waited outside in the corridor. For two days he attempted to follow Iyengar's instructions and movements from his distant vantage point. On the third day, Iyengar came up to him before class and asked why he wasn't in the class itself. When Eric explained, Iyengar asked his students how many of them knew about Eric, and when they replied that they all did, Iyengar told them that they might as well leave the class, apart from Eric, for they were only there to show him how much they knew, but Eric was there to learn. Iyengar then showed Eric how to do the exercises on the floor, since he was unable to walk unaided, and at the end of the course asked him to keep practising and to come back in a year's time.

At the end of the year, Eric went to India to study with Iyengar. 'India changed my life. It was very hard, I was totally off base, but being off base was the secret, because I had no habits to fall back on. I could only learn. At the end of six months I came home a changed person and it started me on my path. I trained with other Iyengar teachers in the LA area and eventually became a certified teacher. Seventeen years ago Iyengar said to me, "Well, now it's time for you to teach, but you

Eric Small likes to meditate on a cushion on a carpet, so the courtyard in the garden just beyond his yoga room (ABOVE) is laid with a rug, depending on the weather. He always places his bell beside him, and the plants chosen for the garden are predominantly pink, to soothe and uplift the heart and spirit.

must only teach what you know yourself, what you've learned from me." I had surgery on my eyes, which restored all but my peripheral vision; until then I was registered as blind. But you learn to see differently, your hearing, touch and smell improve, and you use all that information, you learn to read people's bodies. You sense a problem and instantly know what treatment is required. Iyengar maintains that this is universal love, universal intelligence coming through you and that you've prepared yourself over the years to receive that information and use it properly. When my sight returned, I realised how much work I had to do, because my students needed to be more disciplined. They had got away with too much before, when I was blind!'

Eric meditates both inside and out. Indoors, he sits in front of the fireplace in his yoga room early in the morning. When he left for India for the first time, this space was a private projection room. 'As a child we used to have a projectionist come up and show the latest movies before they came out on release, but when I left for India my wife asked me what I would like to do with the room. I told her that I wanted to make it into a yoga studio and meditation space. She asked me how I wanted it to be, and when I returned, it was exactly as I'd described it!'

It is a masculine room – which Eric says positively oozes with testosterone when he works with his advanced male pupils – but its masculinity is softened by images of Parvati, Shiva's consort, and by the wonderful soft, feminine garden just outside the French windows at one end of the room.

RIGHT AND OPPOSITE: Wherever she happens to be, Hedi Kleinman surrounds herself with images that answer her need to connect with Spirit, both at work and in her home.

AN ARTIST'S RETREATS: LONG ISLAND AND NEW YORK

NEW YORK, USA

Hedi Kleinman

Regardless of physical location, many people surround themselves with images that answer their need to connect with Spirit, whether it is at home or at work.

Hedi Kleinman, the spiritual artist, is one of them. She lives in New York but escapes to East Hampton each summer. Space may be more of an issue in New York City, but out on Long Island she gives each of the spiritual images in her house a proper perspective. Whether it is a small goddess fountain sitting at the end of a long Italianate garden, or a statue indoors, the eye is drawn immediately to each image. Her home in New York is an eclectic mix of all that is meaningful to her spiritually and creatively while the house on Long Island, which has known only three owners since its construction, abounds with images of the Buddha. He can be found in the kitchen watching over the food preparation, and also in the kitchen garden, presiding over the raw ingredients.

'As a painter, I used to describe my painting talent as a gift. But with the advent of spirituality into my life – my spiritual awakening, if you like – I now describe myself as a channel for the sacred in my art.' Hedi meditates every day in one or other of her spaces, but finds that her work is something of a meditation too. 'I see meditation as a need to extend beyond the three-dimensional life we inhabit as humans into an extra dimension of soul, which is our birthright.'

THE TIBET HOUSE
NEW YORK, USA
Robert Thurman and Richard Gere

Buddhism shows a way to live life positively and to the full, by shifting focus from an egocentric world to an international collective of compassionate, enlightened individuals who together can make a difference. It was this belief that led Robert Thurman and Richard Gere, together with a number of other well-known figures including the composer Philip Glass, to found the Tibet House in 1987. It is a space dedicated to preserving the culture of Tibet. Their intention was to provide a forum for Tibet's unique art and culture, to help preserve and restore it and to share its spiritual message with the world. To this end the Tibet House, in collaboration with educational and cultural institutions, runs an innovative programme of extraordinary exhibitions, workshops and conferences that extend humanity's horizons and open up an intercultural dialogue. Richard Gere has been quoted as saying, 'In America we have a very strong Christian and Jewish heritage, one of compassion and altruism, but we have very little that encourages enlightenment. The most important contribution I can make is to sponsor teaching of this kind – *bodhicitta* teachings that touch the heart deeply.'

Since the building is devoted to the spirit of the Tibetan people, it has inevitably become a house of Spirit. Calm, restorative, energising, it is a place of quiet joy and celebration. Because Tibetan Buddhism seeks not to replace but to augment and supplement our own spiritual heritage, whatever it may be, the Tibet House is a sanctuary for anyone of any philosophical, cultural or spiritual persuasion.

RIGHT: A painting by Patrick Scott and a mobile sculpture by Susan Cuffe, which hangs from the skylight, adorn the Quiet Room. The mobile (OPPOSITE) is an abstract rendition of hands in prayer, supplication, petition, intercession and peace. The crystal hearts were added later to symbolise universal love.

THE INTERFAITH CENTRE
COUNTY DUBLIN, IRELAND
Dublin City University

Reuters recently reported that Apcoa Parking UK Limited, which manages the work of 80 traffic wardens in Edinburgh, is negotiating with a company specialising in stress management to provide shamanic meditation classes for its overstressed employees. Similarly, one premier football club in England and several major corporations are now designating certain areas on their premises as quiet spaces. They have found that when use of the 'quiet room' is sanctioned, productivity rises exponentially.

Across the Atlantic in Florida, five volunteers at the Gateless Gate Zen Center provide a meditation and retreat programme at their own expense for prisoners in county and state facilities ranging from the local county jail to Death Row. They have found that upon release, many inmates visit the Gateless Gate to continue meditation practice and donate their time, energy and money to further its work.

Spaces that benefit the larger community in an intimate way are now being considered by a number of educational institutions. About 11 years ago, Dublin City University's Interfaith Centre, which has Roman Catholic, Church of Ireland, Presbyterian, Methodist and Islamic representatives, created a Quiet Room to be available all day to students, staff and the local community alike. A small, circular room, it offers anyone a place in which to reflect, meditate, pray, seek solace and listen to his or her inner spirit.

The shelves in the Quiet Room contain books from every faith and tradition, but there is also a small blank book which has generated an interactive support system within the university. Father John Gilligan, the Catholic priest at the Centre, says that people anonymously write down in its pages what they are feeling, sometimes exploring their most painful experiences, and others rally around, replying to the messages with their own words of support and understanding. He believes that the space has achieved much more than they expected, offering a tool for spiritual and communal growth.

THE ACCELERATED SCHOOL
CALIFORNIA, USA
Tara Guber

In California, the dynamic philanthropist Tara Guber has made the same thing happen at the Accelerated School in South Central Los Angeles. The notion of introducing yoga and meditation into the school curriculum may have seemed at first a trifle quixotic, but it has become a model for other schools to follow. Both staff and students have discovered that when the classroom stills for meditation or yoga, the energy of the space changes completely and the children's work and relationships with others – family, friends, staff and fellow students – improves beyond all recognition. As Tara says, 'Bringing meditation and yoga to inner city children like this is a blessing beyond measure. Watching them transform as they get in touch with their inner mentor is unbelievably rewarding and the results are truly impressive.' Tara is currently raising money to build a House of Spirit on the school campus which will provide yoga, meditation, therapy and a mind-body-spirit library for the children during the day and for the wider community out of school hours.

THE YOGA HOUSE
CALIFORNIA, USA

Tara believes that it is her destiny to bring these immeasurable life skills to as many people as possible. (She rather aptly describes meditation as taking 'time in'.) In addition to her work at the Accelerated School, Tara has built the Yoga House, a serene spiritual sanctuary, on a hill high above Beverly Hills. This is a space devoted to Spirit: the world's leading spiritual teachers hold workshops here. The Yoga House is bordered by a high hedge so that it remains untrammelled by outside stimuli, yet if you walk close to the hedge and look down, the glorious view encompasses the whole

of West Los Angeles. Reflecting pools in the garden, crystals and hand-hewn wooden seats celebrate the anomalous beauty of nature – its simplicity and complexity. Lingam stones represent the deity Shiva. The principal room of the house is glazed on three sides, charging the interior with the energy of light. A deep feeling of calm pervades this room and yet, on setting foot in it, each sense is heightened. Chameleon-like, the space can transform itself for the needs of its users, be it for meditation, yoga, or a quiet supper in cherished company.

This beautiful space seems to represent the Buddhist *enso*, in which the Buddha nature is rendered as a circle – empty, yet complete at the same time. The *enso* contains nothingness and yet it contains everything – for what is it without the space that it encircles and the space that encircles it? The *enso* is a cipher that encourages the realisation of true human potential.

Beyond this room, there is a smaller meditation room and a bedroom. These spaces are inevitably darker and more enclosed. They feel more intimate, more womb-like; they are places for conception or respite. Yet they, too, breathe a stillness and calm which restores the soul and equanimity.

The entire complex is designed to harmonise with the environment around it. The buildings, the reflecting pools, the crystals, the statues, the wooden seats all blend seamlessly with nature, and in the midst of it the Yoga House is literally an encapsulation of Spirit.

ABOVE AND OPPOSITE: Clodagh's core philosophy is to use the elements -
earth to centre her clients in their space, fire to bring living energy
into a room, water to cleanse and uplift the spirit and air to allow free
circulation. She also considers the senses imperative - colour (or lack
of it), texture, scent and music are important in a design.

USING THE NATURAL ELEMENTS
NEW YORK, USA
Clodagh

Most of us feel a sense of connection with a particular space. It may be nostalgia for one that we used to live in, happiness in a place that we currently live in, or yearning for something other than we have at present, without knowing quite what it is that we want. But for some people it is a prerequisite that the whole home should resonate with the sensibility of its owner – thus becoming, in effect, a living, breathing sanctuary.

The designer Clodagh has been an environmentalist since her early youth and this is clearly expressed in all she creates, whether it is a spa in New Zealand or an apartment for Robert Redford in New York. Unlike many other designers or architects, she does not seek to impose her own vision on her client; instead, she attempts to discover exactly what will make her client happy, for as she says, 'A home will never be truly beautiful unless it functions in harmony with who we are.'

Clodagh's philosophy is to use the elements – earth, fire, air and water – and to stay as close to nature as possible, using natural materials, allowing for erosion and, when lighting a room, incorporating shadows, for she believes that lighting without shadow is surreal.

Clodagh refers to herself as a travel consultant, for she takes her clients on an inner journey to find out what is missing in their lives and what will help revive or supply the missing elements in their home environment. She asks her clients to use the four Cs: to Contemplate their current space and tell her how well it functions for them, to Cleanse their lives of any extraneous items, to Clarify their needs and intentions and then to Create the space that is right for them. As Clodagh herself says, 'Your whole home should be a sacred space, a sanctuary. It should live and breathe with you. It should lift your spirits and calm your soul.'

Open

to the

Sky

Open to the Sky
Gardens, Courtyards and other Natural Sanctuaries

For thousands of years gardens have been created as places of peace and sanctuary. A garden is, after all, a celebration of nature's abundance and generosity. Humanity has always looked to nature to better understand the divine, whether within the simplicity of a Zen Garden, the healing energy of a physic garden or the fourfold design of an Islamic garden. The very word 'paradise' comes from the Ancient Greek *paradeisos*, which in turn derives from the Persian meaning 'a walled garden or park'.

Harold Nicholson and Vita Sackville-West understood this implicitly when they created their home at Sissinghurst Castle. They used their garden not as an adjunct to their home, but literally as 'rooms' in which to live, a practice characteristic of the Renaissance garden. The garden next to the Priest House at Sissinghurst, in which they dined, weather permitting, is rectangular and divided by two intersecting paths into four equal sections, with a square at the point where the paths cross. It is typical of Islamic garden design and of Persian garden design in particular.

Whilst the Christian tradition views Paradise as a continuation of the reality of life on earth, the Muslim tradition attempts to recreate Paradise on earth. The Islamic garden not only expresses joy at the bounty and beauty of nature, but also symbolises metaphysical understanding of the workings of the Universe.

The Chinese, who follow the ancient art of Feng Shui, talk of an invisible energy field that they call *chi*, or vital force. But they also talk of *li*, the visible effect of chi. As the aromachalogist, John Steele, puts it, 'Li is the visible manifestation of wind swirling in fields of grain or the rippling patterns of breeze on a lake. It is the organic pattern found in the grain of cypress wood, the petals of a rose, the veins in a piece of jade, the melody of a flute, the flow of water around a rock in a stream, the patterns of your finger tip whorls or the way a beautiful head of hair cascades. It is an innate sense of harmonic form which is often undulatory, asymmetric and never repeats itself exactly,

with infinite variations on a theme.' The li of a sacred space allows us to submerge ourselves in the divine, to physically experience it. The guttering flame as a candle is lit, the harmonic of a note as a singing bowl is sounded, the curl of incense smoke spiralling upward – each is a visual, aural or olfactory prompt to devotion. Gardeners are celebrating both chi and li when they create gardens as sacred spaces.

STORIES IN A GARDEN
GLOUCESTERSHIRE, UK
Ken and Ann Allen

To walk into Ken and Ann Allen's world is to walk into a wonderful
narrative garden which celebrates their life's work. Passionate
gardeners – they have run a group of garden centres since 1984 –
they take you by the hand and show you the extraordinary nature
of Nature itself.

The first garden, designed by Paul Cooper, is based on Jean-
Auguste Dominique Ingres' picture *La Source*. An abstract metal grille represents the painting.
Beneath it, water flows under a curl and curve of slate sloping upwards, like sharp shale, to
represent the twists and turns of life. The slate path leads on to the encircled world, a pool of water
with fish swimming lazily through it, and from under the path the water gurgles into the pool.

Set into the 'river' of shale is a flat square of York stone and at the water's edge, a small wooden
rail at waist height. Standing on this stepping-stone in the middle of the stream of life and
leaning on the 'bridge', you look into the 'world' and contemplate where you are in the process
of creation.

At one side of the pool, two tall pillars support a steel rod balancing large stones with slate
shards – *yin* and *yang*, the female and male principles, dark and light, stillness and animation –
and when a breeze blows, the stones dip into the water, creating ripples, movement and life.
Beyond, plants, mainly hostas, curve away like an estuary towards large abstract structures: a
cube of lead, squares, cones and spheres. It is an eclectic mix, representing modernism – our urge
to manipulate the natural environment artistically and creatively using science and technology.
Ken moves these structures from time to time to signify that there is no set blueprint, for
everything is changeable.

Moving on, you enter an area created by Julie Toll where four figures, again designed by Paul Cooper, and based on drawings by Albrecht Dürer of the human form, embrace a simple granite patio. The figures were originally designed for the Allens' garden centre to remind staff, suppliers and, above all, customers that their philosophy was people-orientated. Beside the patio a metal sheet with a ceramic sphere resting on it mirrors nature and the beholder – a reminder that human beings have the capacity to reflect. It draws you inexorably into the meditation garden beyond.

Although they originally planned the space as an outdoor auditorium to celebrate family life, music and laughter, the Allens decided to use it for meditation after Ann was diagnosed with breast cancer in 1971. As so often in time of crisis, the Allens faced their fear with courage, faith and a search for the meaning of existence. It seemed natural for them to find it in Theravadan Buddhism, an experiential form of Buddhism.

The space is magical for meditating on and in nature. According to Ann, their friends come and sit there regularly, simply to feel the energy of peace. This intimate garden engenders a feeling of sharing and participation. An old oak embraces the space, a yew hedge on three sides protects it, and yet it is also open to the sky. The wooden decking beneath is a reminder that you are sitting on a gift from nature, as you face the statue of Buddha, lit by a gentle dusky glow when the sun dips behind the field beyond. Although it is fairly small and enclosed, when sitting in this peaceful, perfumed space you seem to be caught in infinity.

Next, two figures by Paul Cooper loom over an elliptical courtyard, deep in conversation, a witty reference to Jaques' observation in Shakespeare's *As You Like It* that 'all the world's a stage, and all the men and women merely players'. However, this section of the garden is closest to the house, presenting a witty conundrum: either the garden is a borrowed landscape, the world looking in at us, the actors who inhabit the house; or we, the audience, are looking out at a drama enacted in the garden.

The wilder section of the garden comprises a boardwalk garden, using seemingly unusable space in a ditch, a wood and a wild flower meadow, and in one corner is the most miraculous meditation space of all. Originally conceived as a willow sculpture, with the help of Ewen McEwen this domed space evolved organically. Having planted 29 giant willow cuttings in a circle, with gaps at each side to make 'entrances', Ken and Ann Allen are in the process of grafting the willows together, allowing space for a 'window' on to the meadow beyond. At present it is a beautiful skeleton, but in time the willows will grow strongly together creating a canopy overhead, and the tree meditation space will live on the same roots, with the same sap flowing around each branch. The energy engendered in this cupola is tangible, humbling and awe-inspiring, opening up the flow of life within and around everyone entering it. To sit in the centre and meditate is to feel the energy of the tree and be part of nature itself.

AN EXTRASENSORY GARDEN
BERKSHIRE, UK
Uri Geller

Uri Geller is the world's most celebrated paranormalist and also an author. He made his name in his native Israel and by 1972 was attracting attention across Europe, demonstrating his psychokinetic and telepathic powers. Advisor to some of the world's most influential politicians, scientists and corporations, he has worked with the FBI, CIA and NASA, to name but a few.

At home, Uri Geller has created enclaves throughout his garden where he can feel the right frequencies and be close to ley lines, so that he can connect fully with their energy. He never has any concrete plan for meditation, but each day he chooses a different place in his garden, depending on his mood – more often than not by the waterfall. There is never a day when he is not outside meditating. Whatever the weather, he is there, for he truly feels the five elements of the planet – air, earth, fire, water and wood – in his garden.

Crystals placed throughout the garden, particularly around the waterfall, are there to gather and remit energy. Geller does not believe, as others do, that crystals emanate healing powers, although he does not rule out the possibility that some crystal vibration could enhance healing. He asserts, instead, that they are wonderful tools for transforming the mind. He collects the crystals later and gives them to people who need them.

In the top section of the garden stands a gazebo with a star symbol embedded in the ground. Uri uses this space in a ritualistic way. Standing in the centre of the star, he connects with the symbolism of the planet and transmits his thought waves to someone who needs them, or experiments with extra-sensory perception.

ABOVE AND OPPOSITE ABOVE: The Japanese garden, scattered with amethysts
and (OPPOSITE BELOW) the Star gazebo are just two of the meditation spaces
in Uri's garden. The gazebo is where Geller stood when he famously stopped
the clock of Big Ben, London's famous landmark, in the 1990s.

THE STAR COURTYARD AT SHAMBHALA
SOMERSET, UK
Isis Livingstone

Some sacred places breathe an air of mystery and enchantment. At Shambhala (Sanskrit for 'perfect peace and love'), a retreat centre in Glastonbury, there is a courtyard in the garden known as the Star Courtyard. Isis Livingstone, who owns and runs the centre, recalls how one night during a relentless electrical storm a bolt of lightning, like a column of gold, struck the courtyard outside the house. Realising that they somehow had to utilise the energy created by this freak event, her husband raced out afterwards and marked the spot with a brick. They then set about finding natural quartz crystals from Arizona, each one blessed, and laid them out in a seven-pointed star shape. The crystals are set into the courtyard like a bird's wing, each crystal feathering the next. The effect is astonishing – you feel, when stroking them, as if they would move to your touch.

Three years ago, whilst meditating, Isis sensed that the star should be twelve-pointed, so after experimenting with different permutations, she and her colleague Argon Nixon decided to paint another star, this time five-pointed, in gold in the centre of the seven-pointed star. The resulting energy surge was extraordinary. A visiting *lama* said he had never seen this star before – a five inside a seven – which is traditionally known as the Star of Eloheim.

The courtyard is a favourite spot for meditation. Tao groups, yoga students and shamans all meditate here. Two or three times a month, Argon and Isis hold a gong meditation. The sound of the gong reverberating around the courtyard is magical. These meditations are usually spontaneous. People take off their watches and switch off their mobile phones when they enter Shambhala in order to experience the flow and the flexibility of time, and in doing so, they find that time is given to those who need it.

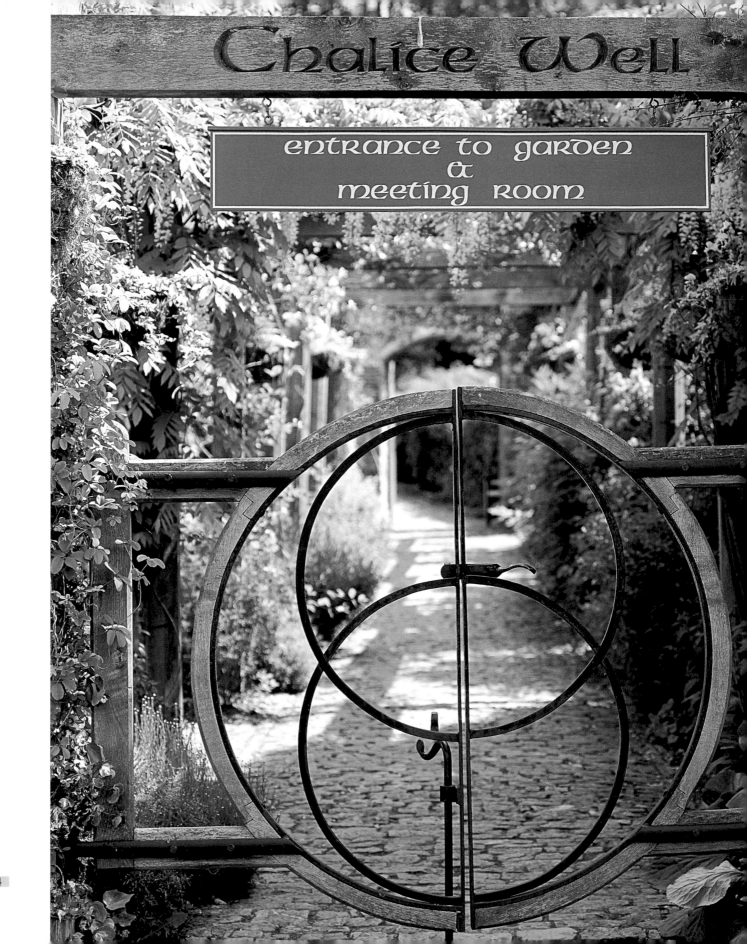

CHALICE WELL
SOMERSET UK
Wellesley Tudor Pole

Chalice Well is Glastonbury's hidden jewel. You could easily walk right past it and not know what you had missed. Yet, step inside, and you become part of a wonderful exclusivity, feeling totally alone when in reality there may be many others around you seeking a quiet moment. A secret garden, it retains a special quality of stillness. When Wellesley Tudor Pole (or 'TP', as he was known) formed the Chalice Well Trust, he wanted to create a sacred space – the garden, with the well at its heart, and the retreat house – that, whilst rooted in the Christian tradition, would be a place of pilgrimage and respite for people from every faith seeking spiritual enlightenment and peace.

The entrance is only four years old, and was designed to let visitors slowly move away from the bustle of the road and town into the sacred space beyond. The planting is all in soft greens and purples and there is an abundance of perfumed plants. Coming away, you can smell the faint waft of curry plant, honeysuckle and jasmine on your clothes. Everywhere you look you see the *vesica piscis*, which became the symbol of Chalice Well about fifteen years ago.

CELTIC CIRCLES AND SPIRALS
COUNTY CARLOW, IRELAND
Jacquie Burgess and Herbie Brennan

Some places on earth seem to teem with time-honoured energy and spiritual awareness: Ireland is one of them. Prehistoric stone circles are scattered across the landscape, and Jacquie Burgess and Herbie Brennan chose to follow that layout when they created a thirteen-stone circle in their own garden. Created to bless the marriage of Herbie's daughter, the circle is now used for meditation, spiral meditation in particular.

Stone circles are usually composed of nine or thirteen stones. The numbers nine and thirteen have magical qualities. Nine is the opposite of one; it reminds us of power or giving power away, that our relationship with Self and the whole cosmos is one of compassion and service. Thirteen is often thought unlucky, perhaps because of the connotation of the Last Supper; but for the Celts it was very lucky indeed, since it represented the lunar cycle by which their lives were ruled.

Herbie and Jacquie planned the circle allowing a space of up to thirteen square feet. Using a pole, a compass and a length of twine, they fixed the pole with the twine attached to the centre of the site, the radius of the circle being determined by the length of twine. They then traced the circumference in silver

sand and, using the compass, marked the positions of the stones.

The recumbent stone, a low, fairly flat stone, was positioned in the south-west, with the portal stones, the two tallest, most upright stones, directly opposite it, marking the entrance to the circle. The remaining ten stones were placed around the circle in descending height order from the portals to the recumbent stone. Jacquie and Herbie then marked out the secondary directions and the twelve months or moons of the year. Again, the portal stones represented one direction.

In the centre of the stone circle, Herbie and Jacquie have mown a spiral for performing spiral meditations. This is an immensely powerful moving meditation which alters an individual's perception of both time and space, transforming reality and opening up inner worlds. Best done blindfold for maximum effect, following the spiral into the centre, with a guiding hand to help, gives you the sensation of undertaking a long journey and covering an immense amount of ground. Reaching the centre and standing on the threshold between the upper and lower worlds, you effectively become the point at which the two worlds join and consequently your vision opens. When ready, you remove your blindfold and retrace your steps, carrying your new knowledge and understanding back into the world.

ST CLARE'S GARDEN
CALIFORNIA, USA
The Sisters of St Clare

Water is rich in symbolism. It is the source of life, representing the flow of time, signifying birth and the hope of new life; it is used to cleanse and give absolution. Water is the most important feature in Islamic gardens and in the gardens of the Taoists, for whom everything in nature has its own spirit. Water is also the most significant element in St Clare's Garden, a beautiful series

of gardens and enclosures created by the Sisters of St Clare, an order of Roman Catholic nuns.

Inspired by St Francis of Assisi and St Clare, after whom the order is named, they set about creating a sacred space in Brea, California. Initially, back in 1990, the task they set themselves seemed impossible, and yet somehow they were able to buy land and were given support to make it happen. As Sister Briegeen says, 'There was a hunger and thirst for this space. It simply evolved.'

There are five gardens in all, each featuring water, and a small chapel where everyone is welcome. The Reflection Garden, which greets the visitor first, is based upon the Japanese principle of harmony and balance. Large stones provide structure and stability; the water, which runs from north to south, is quiet and yielding. A bridge stretches across the water to the porch beyond.

The Herbal Garden is a physic garden, brimming with medicinal and culinary herbs to heal the mind, body and soul. At the west end lies the courtyard, a cool, restful spot with a well in one corner. Wells were placed in gardens and sanctuaries to symbolise a deepening of the inner self towards a conscious communication with God.

The other gardens each have a different purpose. The Childhood Garden explores the inner child, with swings and hopscotch, ladders, bird-houses and a tree-house. Beyond lies the Garden of Living Waters, where falling water cascades over huge boulders into small catching pools and the air is thick with butterflies from the Butterfly Grotto, an area planted with buddleia and bougainvillea to attract these jewel-like insects. The newest garden to emerge is the Peace Garden, with a pavilion, loosely modelled on a Japanese tea-house, bordering a long, shallow pool. This area is particularly popular with meditators and pilgrims, for it invites them to stretch out, slow down, be still ... and contemplate.

STEPPING-STONES

NEW YORK, USA *Peter Mathiessen*
CALIFORNIA, USA *Eric Small*

It is not just the sanctuary garden that is important: often the path leading to it serves a purpose too. The stepping-stones leading up from the road to Peter Mathiessen's *Zen do* were donated by Peter's neighbour. 'He never comes to the Zen do himself, but he wished to honour the space in some way, so he ordered the stones and had them delivered. Then I laid them up to the door of the Zen do. I don't know what the Chinese glyph by the gate represents, but it seemed right to put it there.'

Eric Small's garden begins outside in the street, bordered by a series of chakra stepping-stones which Eric himself laid down. The stones symbolise the path from the outside world into a spiritual oasis. The first stone, which represents the base chakra, by chance resembles the symbol for yin and yang and it draws you, via the other six stones, into a peaceful, meditative space. The garden, just beyond Eric's meditation room, was created by a student of his as an expression of gratitude. Eric loves to sit here in the evening to meditate, or in one of four other places in his six-acre garden. 'My wife always asks me why I meditate outside, since I always close my eyes, and I tell her that when I close my eyes, I carry this image in my mind and the image takes me through the breath into the meditation. My physical eyes may be closed, but my third eye is open.'

Each one of these sacred gardens reminds us that everything in our world is miraculous – whether we look at ourselves and marvel at the infinite capacity of the human body to repair and regenerate, or look around us at the extraordinary interconnectedness of everything in nature. It is easy to forget that we rely on plants for oxygen, just as plants in turn rely on animals for the carbon dioxide they need to breathe. It is easy to forget, too, that life on earth is tied to the cyclical rhythms of the seasons, the tides and the tilt of the planet as it moves around its sun. Our hunger for a stronger connection with nature has led to a renewed interest in Native American traditions and beliefs, which see earth – Gaia – as the sacred mother, a living organism that sustains all. Sitting still in these garden sanctuaries reminds us that we have so little time here on Earth to show our love of life, nature, family, friends – and if we are not careful, we waste it.

ABOVE: The utter simplicity of Zen is inherent in the
gateway to Peter Matthiesen's Zen do. A small pile
of stones, a rustic gate and a circular Chinese glyph
invite the visitor to step on to the path beyond.

A Womb

within

a Room

A Womb within a Room
Shelters, Tents and Enclosures

Today's world is so fast and frenetic that we tend to live in a state of constant expectation. We rail at our cars if they do not set off at the turn of a key. We fly across the world without thinking twice. We blame anyone other than ourselves when we come up against a technological problem we are not equipped to solve. The mystery seems to have been taken out of our lives – and every one of us likes to explore the hidden, the mysterious. If the truth were told, most of us crave a spiritual centre – we may have substance, but do we have enough soul? Perhaps this is why so many people long for a place where they can simply *be*. It may be small or large, a tent or a chapel – what matters is that it is a space for silence, a space for inspiration, a space for solace.

Carl Jung and Vita Sackville-West both sought seclusion in towers. Indeed, Vita laid claim to the Tower at Sissinghurst Castle and no-one dared ascend the stairs without her prior permission. It was her private domain, her writing room, her sanctuary. Jung apparently retreated to his tower to think, to dream and to paint. The walls of his tower rooms are covered in paintings, which speak of possible out-of-body experiences. Jung's house, round and built near water, is an embodiment of his beliefs. It took him twelve years to complete the four quarters of the building, which resembles a *mandala* with a central tower. When finished, he described it in *Memories, Dreams, Reflections* as 'a symbol of psychic wholeness'.

Whilst many people feel the urge to explore Spirit through their gardens or to devote whole rooms or buildings to their relationship with the divine, others prefer more intimate spaces. It may be that they feel more comfortable in a smaller space, or they find that they are hampered by financial constraints or lack of space .

There are many ways of creating sacred space. For some, a corner of a room or a windowsill suffices; others need a space designed specifically for the purpose. It could be a tiny room, perhaps a tent, perhaps even a cupboard ...

A MEDITATION CUPBOARD
CALIFORNIA, USA
Gurmukh

The room in which Gurmukh, a Kundalini yoga teacher, chooses to meditate in her house in Los Angeles is a tiny converted cupboard. 'I knew that I needed a space where I could be undisturbed. This is the only place in the house where I can be just me, alone, meditating, because we are always having people to stay. I pull down the curtain and everyone else knows not to disturb me. It is extraordinary how this small curtain cuts out any extraneous noise. I just close myself off and meditate. When we moved to this house my husband told me that he really didn't want me to bring all my bric-a-brac, so some of the images I have in this room are just postcards, some are small messages or pictures printed off the computer. Some I have had for years, like the pictures of the Madonna and child.'

Every wall is covered with images that resonate with her sensibility. Gurmukh specialises in yoga during pregnancy, so many of her pictures are of goddesses or celebrate motherhood – including one of a Tibetan woman who had three husbands and countless children. 'When you hang out with the Tibetans you never remember the men, only the women. They are strong and powerful without being overbearing.'

For Gurmukh, her whole home is an extension of her work. 'On Sundays, our living area is filled with people. All our students are welcome. Everyone gathers and eats and talks. They just come. That is what the house is for – companionship and celebration. In the west, families have broken down, homes have disintegrated, people don't feel they belong anywhere. But if they feel they belong

to a home, a family, or just a small unit of friends, then they will thrive.'

Throughout the house, Gurmukh has hung collages of the women whose babies she has seen through pre-natal yoga. It is a celebration of her work and her philosophy. She says that she loves to see women, some stressed, anxious, perhaps even angry about their pregnancy because it interferes with their professional plans, eventually soften and accept their situation as expectant mothers.

But the predominant feature of Gurmukh's house is the proliferation of spiritual images. The eclectic mix represents her odyssey from Christianity to Sikhism. There are mandala pictures from the Himalayas, Buddhist altars from Ladakh, sandalwood sculptures of Ganesh, Hanuman and Kuan Yin, sculptures from Maui, statues of the Madonna and the Lady of Fatima, pictures of Jesus, and township dolls from South Africa.

'In India, creating sacred space in your home is normal. Your scriptures, your altar are an integral part of the home. Everything in my home reminds me of the Creator. I like to see images of the godlike or of creative inspiration. I move the statues around all the time, since I like to feel an interactive relationship with God. My husband is content to look at the same thing year in and year out, but my altars change almost every week. I love India because there is a devotion there that has endured for thousands and thousands of years. In the West we do not have that same devotion to the Divine, but I attempt to achieve it here.'

When Kenneth Thompson first discovered the
ice house (ABOVE LEFT), there were stalactites
dripping from the ceiling, and four feet of earth
needed to be excavated before he could create
his vaulted chapel (BELOW LEFT AND OPPOSITE).

TWO HOMES,
TWO CHAPELS
COUNTY CORK, IRELAND
Kenneth Thompson

The stone sculptor Kenneth Thompson has built two chapels in his family homes. The first was almost accidental. He literally stumbled across a hole in the ground and discovered an 18th-century ice house which he converted into an underground chapel. When he moved to his current home, an old farm on the west coast of Ireland, bordering on the Atlantic Ocean and built around a beautiful courtyard, he set about renovating the outbuildings to create studios and workshops, finishing with a tiny oratory in the north corner. 'When you work in stone, you begin with something untouched and gradually uncover and reveal, releasing the form out of the block. You subtract rather than add to expose the beauty of the natural material. That is why I found the renovation of the buildings and the creation of my chapel so absorbing and rewarding.'

A practising Roman Catholic, Kenneth loves orthodox spirituality and in creating the other chapel, which is only about 12 foot wide and long, he has created an almost Greek orthodox purity. The chapel has rudimentary whitewashed plastering with rounded edges, and two small, unglazed, arched windows made of Portland stone, which he designed and made himself, high up on the walls. For Kenneth, practicality is sacrificed to the aesthetic, for he finds comfort in the beauty of simplicity. 'I'd originally intended to glaze the windows – I actually made the rebates

68

ABOVE AND OPPOSITE: The stained glass panel
in the door of the oratory was originally made for the
ice house chapel. Kenneth moved it from there to shed
light into the tiny chapel attached to his house.

to put the glass in – but I love to feel the wind blowing gently into the chapel and to hear the crash of the sea and the faint birdsong, so I've decided to leave them untouched.'

The stained glass in the door was commissioned from his friend Patrick Pye for the original chapel, but it seemed to belong better in the second one, so he installed it there instead. The only other adornments are a beautiful crucifix given to him by Pye, a kneeler and chair, candles, the flowers that he brings into the chapel each day and an inscription in Purbeck stone to Our Lady. It is the beginning of the *Salve Regina*, carved by Kenneth in Latin. It translates, 'Hail Holy Queen, Mother of Mercy, Hail Our Life, Our Sweetness and Our Hope.' As Kenneth himself says, 'I love beautiful letter

forms. When carving this inscription it became real, an incarnation. I see the oratory as a presence generating a kind of energy. A silent prayer is being offered up all the time here for my family, for my friends, for the world, even when the chapel is empty.'

Kenneth never uses incense or sound in his chapel; he relishes silence, save for the faint sounds of nature. 'I always light the candles, even if they gutter a bit in the breeze, and I say a prayer. I like to come here every morning and evening if I can. I would like to spend half an hour here each time, but even if it's a minute or two, it's enough. I respond so fully to the emptiness of this space, I feel such a sense of freedom here – freedom and peace.'

Simple Buddhist images grace the Zen do (OPPOSITE AND PAGE 64) and its garden (RIGHT). The altar (OPPOSITE) is a drum table designed and made by Hans Hokanson, who also made the wooden platforms.

A ZEN DO ON LONG ISLAND
NEW YORK, USA
Peter Mathiessen

As you drive into Peter Mathiessen's home, you pass a stone garden under construction and beneath the porch by the front door stands a wonderful whale-head skeleton, which Peter found while out beachcombing. When the writer first moved to Long Island, the land was wooded, secluded and relatively untouched. The property included a three-bedroomed house, a workhouse and a stable block which, with the help of the late Hans Hokanson, became a beautiful Zen do and adjoining meditation space. Hans Hokanson made the floor platforms, the altar tables and a ceremonial stake, but in making the Zen do, both men were careful to preserve many of the stable's original features and thus its architectural integrity, whilst creating a serene Buddhist meditation space and ceremonial room.

Peter and Hans, both staunch practising Buddhists, built the Zen do because there was a need for it – both for them personally, for their work and for the wider community on Long Island. Anyone can come into the Zen do any time, any day. Peter says that he has no idea who many of his visitors are; he sees cars parked outside and they just arrive, to experience the tranquillity and to pray or meditate. 'Hans' spirit is strong both here and in the garden, where you can see some of his sculptures. It is a peaceful, restorative space but it is also ceremonial – we inducted a student last week. We shaved his head and honoured him as the Buddha. There are always flowers in the Zen do. One of my students has a garden and comes every day to arrange the flowers, which is a good meditation in itself.'

THE BRIGID CHAPEL AND TEMPLE ROOM
SOMERSET, UK
The Avalon Foundation

Off a courtyard in Glastonbury, a town renowned for its connections with Spirit, are two marvellous spaces donated to the public and tended by the Avalon Foundation. In the corner of a courtyard, so unobtrusive as to be almost overlooked, stands a truly beautiful space, the Brigid Chapel – beautiful because of its utter simplicity.

The chapel has been there for a number of years and is open at all times. The intention is that it should be for young and old alike, of all faiths and beliefs. It is used for occasional hand fasts (about four a year), and for meditation, but mostly it is a pilgrimage site or peaceful haven where anyone can stop and contemplate or sit quietly for a few minutes. The Brigid Chapel is unadorned and non-denominational, so any gift left for the goddess is moved elsewhere.

The Temple Room, on the other hand, literally overflows with gifts left by grateful visiting meditators. Reached by a flight of wooden stairs and a winding spiral staircase, it is a tiny temple at the top of a Georgian building. People think of it very much as a birthing room, where ideas are formulated, movements are founded, and meditation groups find their root. It is a womb-like space – perhaps that is why it gives all those who enter a sense of security and comfort. The Avalon Foundation meditates in this room regularly, as do many other groups.

Diane Von Furstenberg
practises yoga and
meditates each day,
either in the meditation
tent (RIGHT) or on the
roof of her building.
OPPOSITE: A beautiful,
simple wooden sculpture of
the hand in the chin *mudra*.

A TENT FOR MEDITATION
NEW YORK, USA
Diane Von Furstenberg

Diane Von Furstenberg's very first urge on waking is to meditate for about one-and-a-half hours, a practice she was taught by Deepak Chopra when she became ill. Without it she feels deprived and is prone to tension headaches. She finds her meditation is deeper in an enclosed, silent space such as her meditation tent, but says that she can meditate anywhere – on a beach, out walking, even in the swimming pool!

'Solitude and silence is very important to me, because I'm surrounded by noise and activity,' she says. This is literally true, for her private space is located above her thriving fashion design and retail business. 'I believe that meditation acts as a buffer between the conscious and the subconscious which creates resistance and protection, and my meditation spaces serve the same function. Whilst meditation for me is like a prayer – I use the word *reculer* (a French word meaning "to retreat, step back, withdraw") – yoga makes me more aware of myself and my capabilities. It gives me control and strength and complicity with the Self. Both yoga and meditation are all about focus, centring and stability.'

THE SANCTUARY ROOM

SOMERSET, UK

Isis Livingstone

Glastonbury is a cornucopia of hidden spaces, simple, beautiful, quiet, still. At Shambhala, Isis Livingstone recounts how, when she first bought her property, which clings to the edge of Glastonbury Tor, she began creating meditative spaces at the top of the building, slowly moving down the house, and it seemed to evolve organically.

She first created the Sanctuary room, dedicated to Mary and the Seven Suns. It is a space of infinite peace and light which seems to flow in from above and permeate every inch of the tented space. The room is predominantly blue with touches of white – the cushions, the carpet, the ceiling under the swathes of fine lawn above your head. Even the painting of Mary is blue, yet Mary and the stars appear three-dimensional; they seem to come out of the canvas to greet you.

The garden and dovecote outside are home to Isis' doves, which sit and coo gently on the roof above and along each of the windowsills. Sitting in this room is like sitting in the sky – the tented ceiling barely conceals the vivid blue beneath and light filters into the room from windows on both sides.

The room seems to encourage the most intimate of moments. Isis says that for many of her guests it is a room that immediately restores the equilibrium, a small haven that is often sought out when solace is needed. She recalls how a scholar from America who had done a great deal of research on Mary came to the centre determined to dedicate a space to her – but on seeing the Sanctuary Room, realised that there was no need, for Mary was already palpably evident there.

One end of the Upper Room (ABOVE) is given over to a
small meditation area. At the other end (OPPOSITE),
a wooden table is permanently laid for thirteen,
to celebrate TP's vision of the Last Supper.
The effect, simple in the extreme, is profound.

THE UPPER ROOM
SOMERSET, UK
Wellesley Tudor Pole

Linking the world and the garden at Chalice Well in Glastonbury is the retreat house, with its extraordinary Upper Room. When Wellesley Tudor Pole (known as 'TP') renovated the retreat house, he felt that this room should be a link between the physical and the spiritual planes. At one end a window looks out over the town towards Wearyall Hill, the long, low hill to the south-west where Joseph of Arimathea is believed to have come and planted his staff, and from which a thorn tree grew that is endemic in the Middle East but in the UK is unique to Glastonbury. At the other end, a window looks up at the Tor – a steep-sided hill shrouded in myth.

In one of his most powerful visions, TP saw the events leading up to the Last Supper, and he set out to recreate the upper room exactly as he saw it in his vision. Great efforts were made to find historically accurate materials, so everything on the table is wood, save for the clay pitchers, the amphorae and the rush matting on the floor. TP's attention to detail was legendary: he glazed the windows with yellow glass to give the look of a setting Mediterranean sun and placed a lamp in one window which is lit at all times to welcome visitors and light the way for passers-by.

Religious ceremonies are not held in the Upper Room, but meditation has taken place there for thirty-three years. It is intended as a place in which to sit down and let go. You come to the Upper Room with a problem, step inside and leave your troubles outside the door, opening yourself up and offering a prayer of love and healing. No single religious group practises meditation here. It represents a threshold between the physical, causal plane and the spiritual, non-physical realm. The room is a place for silence, a room for Everyman, and consequently the atmosphere is imbued with vibrant energy and light.

A JAPANESE TEA-HOUSE IRISH STYLE
COUNTY CORK, IRELAND
Stephen Pearce

The Japanese tea-house built by the potter Stephen Pearce has evolved as a sacred space over a period of 47 years. When Stephen was eleven, he planted the trees that now surround the thatched house, knowing that he wanted to make a connection with spirit and with nature. It was only thirty years later that he realised he needed to create his space of Spirit and nature among the trees he had planted. 'Like a cake that cooks very slowly, this space could not be rushed: it needed to evolve in its own time.'

As Stephen set about building the tea-house, he took care not to cut down any trees. Whilst he employed a team to build the structure, each day he sat and meditated on the space and let the detail somehow flow out of him. The result is that sitting in this space, it is as if you are floating in air. Huge windows on each side look out through the trees down to a lake, on which he has created an island, and out over the landscape of Shanagarry. It gives an impression of seclusion, even though it is only about one hundred metres from his home and pottery.

The tea-house is an exotic mix of Irish and Japanese influence. The roof pitch corresponds to a thatched

Japanese roji, but the thatching technique is Irish. The ceilings are made of cedarwood, whose gentle scent induces an immediate sense of relaxation. Timber floors and whitewashed walls are adorned with gold on backgrounds of natural linen, huge abstract paintings by Patrick Scott and some cushions, the only vibrant colour being the flowers that Stephen's wife brings into the tea-house each day. It is a space that palpably breathes silence and peace; it invites you to enter the stillness. Stephen and his wife meditate regularly in the house, but they also got married here, so it is also a place of celebration, exuding a quiet joy.

'I come here to get away from work, to empty my mind and see what comes in. My best ideas seem to come to me here, which is why I have created a space like this in each of my homes. But this particular space is very special – it is contained and yet, when you step inside, it gives the impression of infinite space and a unique closeness to nature. Even the wild animals have adopted it as their own; the herons come and shelter against the glass in winter to feel the warmth within on their feathers.'

Elise Frick's shrine room (ABOVE) is simple
and uncluttered yet sumptuous and elegant,
partly due to the wonderful quality
of light that floods through the
tall French windows (OPPOSITE).

A TIBETAN-STYLE SHRINE ROOM

NEW YORK, USA

Elise Frick

When Elise Frick acquired her building on Lexington Avenue, she instantly felt that it would be interesting to have a shrine room in it. The room that she ultimately created is a sanctuary – tranquil and unpretentious. Even with French windows open to the garden below, the noise of the city traffic is somehow diminished. During a turbulent few years of decoration, renovation and tenancy disputes, this room has proved, literally, to be a godsend for residents and landlady alike.

It is a beautiful space. 'The altar has been pretty much the same since I set it up. I was given the *stupa* just last year by a visiting Tibetan lama,' says Elise. A soft white shawl is draped over a picture of the Buddha, seven Tibetan offertory bowls filled with water are set along the front of the shrine together with a mandala, and flowers and plants give life to the room. 'The space has been developing slowly, almost imperceptibly. It has a gentle energy which grows subtly day by day. Everyone who comes into the building feels it. The shrine room has changed the building itself: it is full of a quiet joy.'

Elise is currently studying the Tibetan language at Columbia University so that she can better understand the dynamics of Tibetan Buddhism. 'I use the shrine room at least once a day. Sometimes I meditate, sometimes I just come to sit and be. It is available for anyone to use, whether they live in the building or not. After all, that is its purpose – to serve as a space for quiet reflection for people of any spiritual persuasion.'

The only items in Nitya's sweat-lodge
(LEFT AND OPPOSITE) are the Buddha, which is visible
as you bend to enter through the low, rustic door,
and the Finnish stove that heats the space.

A NATIVE NORTH AMERICAN SWEAT-LODGE
NORFOLK, UK
Nitya

Nitya found his inspiration in North America. While staying on a reservation, he dreamed that he was staying at Mese Verde and met the Hopi goddess known as the Spider Woman. Returning home, Nitya decided to construct a sweat-lodge-cum-meditation room, a womb-like building close to Mother Earth similar to the Native American Indian sweat-lodges or 'hogans'.

It is a building of simplicity and beauty, built in the curve of an apple tree. Normally a North American sweat-lodge would be dark, but Nitya let a window into the roof in order to see the apple tree and sky above; however, a shutter can be pulled across the window to block out the light.

The cabin is made from sycamore, given to Nitya by a local woodsman. Steel rods were placed in each corner of a concrete slab and the sycamore poles, stripped of their bark, were laid on to the rods in a log cabin formation but in an octagonal shape. The floor was tanked several times, then plastered and concreted and decking was laid over the top.

In winter Nitya uses the sweat-lodge roughly once a week, and in summer once a month. 'The physical act of sitting and sweating is a different kind of letting go. On a similar principle, the Tibetans used to sit in the snow in order to leave their bodies behind. In such places it is easy to find an empty space and it is almost impossible to have a normal dialogue in your head. In meditation, you are very sensitive to gravity – you feel the space intensely – so being high in the air or low to the ground intensifies the experience. Meditating in an aeroplane is an incredible experience because the spirit is so light, but when you meditate in or near the ground, as I do in my sweat-lodge, your body merges with its surroundings.'

Nitya loves to meditate, but with his busy schedule – running a mail order herb business with three qualified herbalists plus his wife, the herbalist Jill Davies – he cannot always be at his sweat-lodge, so he has learned to meditate not just here, but anywhere.

A MEDITATIVE WORKPLACE
NORFOLK, UK

Carol and Chris Rudd

The numismatist Chris Rudd and his wife, Carol, a flower essence therapist, follow a more mystic path. They wish to escape *chaurasi*, the endless Hindu cycle of birth and rebirth. Chris believes that he will never find permanent happiness in this realm; the more he tries to go inside himself, the better and happier he feels – and that is a great inducement to meditate. He travels further on his inner journey than any intergalactic traveller. Chris is quick to point out that this is not the preserve of any particular sect, guru or religion – the journey is the same for anyone who meditates – but not everyone may feel the same isolation, the same degree of separation from Source. Carol quotes the mystic, Jalaluddin Rumi, who once remarked, "Why seek the gifts, when you can have the giver?"

For Chris to meditate peacefully, he prefers as little stimulation as possible. His meditation room is therefore sparse, spare and undecorated. He likes to meditate before dawn, when it is still dark and the world is still. Chris first makes himself comfortable; he takes a cup of black tea into his meditation room to wake himself up and opens the window to let in fresh air. He does this to keep himself awake; the room offers him a gateway to greater awareness, not an excuse to drift into oblivion.

The room contains a simple wing-backed chair, a heater, because he meditates all year round, a prayer hat to keep the draught from his head, a shelf hinged against the wall, an inspirational book, a blank book, and a skull above the door to remind him of the impermanence of life. There is also,

rather unusually, a clock, in case he meditates for too long or – more often – not long enough.

If, when Chris enters the room, his head is teeming with thoughts, he puts them straight down on paper in the blank book. Sometimes he writes verse; sometimes he draws cartoons, one of himself asking a question, and one of his master responding. The simple process of writing his thoughts down rids his mind of them. When he feels still, he begins to meditate – usually for two or three hours each day, but sometimes for only one. Most of his meditation is devoted to silently repeating a mantra in order to withdraw his consciousness from the extremities of his body and concentrate it instead at the third eye centre. He may then release the hinged shelf, place his elbows on it and, resting his head in his hands, listen for the sound of silence, the so-called 'music of the spheres'.

Chris describes his meditation room as his real workplace. He says that this may sound ruthlessly practical and unromantic, but he believes that he produces his most important work in this room, and the more practice he puts in, the clearer is his vision and the greater his potential. If he scrimps on his meditation, he feels ill at ease in his body and off-balance for the rest of the day and it is then that he is prone to make foolish decisions.

By focusing on the inner eye, Carol and Chris hope to fulfil their spiritual destiny and complete the journey; their intention is to return to Source. As Chris so eloquently puts it, 'God breathes out and creates, God breathes in and we return to him.'

Gateways

to the

Divine

Gateways to the Divine
Shrines and Altars

As a child, did you have a secret place that you loved to go to? Did you find a place where you could escape from your parents; somewhere that they never knew about, somewhere that was yours alone? Did you fill it with little talismans that you collected? Perhaps there was an acorn, a thrush's egg, a broken piece of china, a glass bottle, a feather or some driftwood from the beach. Did you go there alone, or did you sometimes take a trusted friend to share it with you?

As children, we build ourselves altars and create meaningful spaces without even realising we are doing so! As adults, we do the same. Every home has an altar of some kind – often a mantelpiece or table with photographs of the family and some treasured possessions. However, for some, a shrine or altar is a statement of intent: a focus for celebration or remembrance or a centre for meditation.

When someone creates an altar or shrine, they are literally forging a relationship with the divine; they are giving the sacred a physical form and shape, sometimes using the most ordinary and commonplace of materials. It may be that they wish to energise a space for a specific purpose or person, or to create a peaceful place where they can communicate with a force greater than themselves. Whatever their intention, the ultimate purpose of the altar is to cultivate mindfulness, the awareness of awareness itself.

A shrine can be anywhere – in the kitchen, in the bedroom, under a flight of stairs; indeed, it does not even need to be visible when it is not in use. Amarjeet Bhamra, a Sikh and Indian head masseur, practises from home. His clients come from many walks of life and follow many different faiths. Amarjeet keeps his shrine on a small tray, which he places in a cupboard whilst he is working. 'In this way, whilst I am myself aware that my connection to the divine is very close by, I do not upset or distract my clients' sensibilities.'

The palmist and astrologer Lori Reid is adamant that when setting up a shrine, altar or meditation space, its location should be intuitive. A personal space is just that – personal. It must feel right. It should speak to you on every level. There are good and bad spots in and around the home; anywhere your cat sits regularly is usually a negative geophysical space, so Lori urges the use of a pendulum or simply your own instinct to dowse for the right spot.

When Lori's father died, she was unable to attend his funeral, but she needed to mourn his loss. She rambled around her house and garden feeling miserable until she finally collapsed on a stone trough in the corner of her garden, which felt right, for it somehow brought her solace and became her personal space.

'In Italy, where I was born, every street corner and Catholic home has a shrine or an icon, a statue or picture of a saint. Fresh flowers are placed on the shrines every day. It is very important to have that visible connection with the divine as a constant in your life. You can make your own shrine. It doesn't need a holy relic or statue to be divine; it can have a piece of driftwood or a handful of shells and the shrine can be made from a shoe-box, but as long as it is created with the right intent, it will hold the sacred within it.'

On the whole, people tend to make altars or shrines when they have experienced moments of crisis, but sometimes their creation is a spontaneous gesture of connection to the universe. This is often true of children, who have a natural and ingenuous sense of the divine.

Michael Young has made his own altar at home. His mother says, 'Children learn by example, and my son has grown up with altars and daily devotions around the house, so he soon wanted to create his own.' Michael began by finding a small ornamental table and cleaning it. Next, he collected pictures of spiritual teachers and arranged them amongst religious artefacts that he treasures: a Ganesh statue from India, some small Buddha figurines, a framed miniature of His Holiness the Dalai Lama, a pendant of Mother Mary from one of Mother Theresa's nuns, a small bible and prayer book from a Catholic priest and family friend, a lucky symbol from a Japanese temple, a crucifix from a Greek Orthodox church dedicated to Saint Michael and a Tibetan *mala* (prayer beads) for reciting

mantras, given to him by a visiting Tibetan Lama. Michael then added elements from nature: intriguingly-shaped rocks found on beaches or mountains and brought home 'for God', a bird's feather, some shells and crystals, a favourite glass marble, some candles, an incense-holder and a box of cards with angel quotations.

Michael often lights incense or burns a candle on the altar. Sometimes he recites prayers or mantras and rearranges the objects there, and he loves to offer the box of angel cards to visitors and friends so that they can choose one and find their own message or guardian angel. As his mother explains, 'The altar is his way of exploring his connection with the Divine and expressing his delight in natural beauty. But it also functions in times of crisis. When someone dies, he puts their picture on it and makes offerings of sweets or toys to focus his thoughts and prayers. The altar helps him accept their passing and makes him feel he is helping them. But it is primarily a place of celebration, because even the gods get a piece of his birthday cake!'

A SHRINE ROOM FOR CORPORATE USE

NEW YORK, USA

Barbara Corcoran

Barbara Corcoran, founder and head of the Corcoran real estate group in New York, quotes her mother whenever she feels the need to unwind. 'She simply says to me, "Stop! What were you worrying about this time last year?" It immediately puts everything back into perspective and I begin to intuit the answer to my problem.' Barbara firmly believes that intuition and feelings play a major role in the success of her corporation, because people buy homes with their heart first and then with their head.

It was this approach that prompted her, when she moved into her new office headquarters in Manhattan in 1997, to first 'smudge' the entire building (smudging is a Native North American tradition of space-clearing and purifying) then to have it looked at by a Feng Shui expert, and finally to create a prosperity shrine. As she puts it, 'Truth lies in feeling rather than in logic, so it was not a conscious decision to change the workspace – it was intuition at work. I thought, why not try it? It can only add to the energy in the workspace, or do nothing at all.' Her judgement has proved to be one hundred per cent accurate, because the success of the Corcoran Group increased exponentially from then on!

As Scott Durkin , the chief executive officer, says, 'We don't expect everyone who works here to buy into this philosophy, but the shrine represents a peaceful space where people can come and just sit and relax. It is a tranquil spot in a frenetic environment, but it is also a place of celebration. The atmosphere in here holds and restores you.'

RIGHT: Philip Anthony always burns incense, lights candles and puts candy and fruit out on his altar, both as offerings to the gods and for his clients. Like Michael Young, he likes to move each item around so that the altar takes on a life of its own.

A SURFBOARD SHRINE

NEW YORK USA

Philip Anthony

It is rare to meet people who make offerings of food on their altars, although in Mexico it is customary to make altars for the Day of the Dead, when ancestors are honoured with feasting and festivity. On these altars a family will place flowers, gifts and, most important of all, the favourite food of the deceased relative. However, Philip Anthony, a practitioner of osteokinetics in New York who is currently writing a thesis on traditional Chinese medicine, also never forgets to place sweets and fruit on his shrine. He is a devotee of the Hawaian and Polynesian custom of building a new shrine on the beach each week, using driftwood, pebbles, shells and flowers. His home and his shrines strongly reflect his passions – for fatherhood, for *tiki* (pseudo-Polynesian artwork), for Chinese medicine, and for surfing.

Each of his shrines is constructed around a surfboard. As he puts it, 'I'd rather surf than anything else, because if I'm not strenuously using my body, then it feels as if part of my inner medicine is missing.' His main altar reflects numerous religions and other strong influences. It holds images of Jesus, the Buddha, Ganesh, bowls of Chinese herbs and fertility symbols, for he and his partner are hoping to have a child.

Every surface in Kathy Jones's house is a potential altar to the Goddess.
Wherever the eye falls, there is an image of her and this is what Kathy loves.
Whether it is (ABOVE) the Three in One - the Maiden-Mother-Crone - or
(OPPOSITE, TOP SHELF) a Black Tara, by filling her vision with a goddess image,
Kathy is conscious of her at all times.

IMAGES OF THE GODDESS
SOMERSET, UK
Kathy Jones

Kathy Jones, founder of the Goddess Conference in the UK, has always been a keen spiritual seeker. As a youngster in Wales, she found all religions patriarchal but with the advent of feminism, the split between masculine religions and life passions became strong in her. She travelled to Glastonbury to do full moon meditations and eventually moved there. She recounts how, one extraordinary night during a protest against nuclear weapons at Greenham Common, she realised, as she sang along with the other protestors, that she was referring to the Spirit as She. It was a revelation. The Spirit had always been He to Kathy before, but now the Spirit was feminine, so she started to learn about the Goddess. She began by finding what had existed in the past in terms of feminine spirituality and then recreated it in the present, by rewriting ancient myths for the theatre. She quickly found that people's lives were changed by these sacred dramas – not just hers, but those of all who participated.

Kathy describes herself as a mythographer. She wants to tell myth but change it by bringing past knowledge into the present, to create the kind of world that she and, hopefully, others would like to see. Her aim is to redeem the feminine first, and then bring in the masculine to complement and balance it. Myth, to her, is creating a picture or story that shows the laws of nature. She believes that whilst the laws of nature govern the physical world, there are psychic laws, too, which create the mythic layer and drive much of human behaviour. If we are to change as human beings, we have to change at the mythic level, but first we must know and understand what it is.

Kathy Jones's home is a simple house in a busy Glastonbury street, which, on entering, becomes a paean to the Goddess. Goddess images are dotted amongst photographs of her family, in company with a bottle of whisky on a table in the corner, scattered throughout the garden, in pictures, on the floor – everywhere.

A CHAKRA ALTAR
CALIFORNIA, USA
Paul Heussenstamm

As you enter the sacred room in Paul Heussenstamm's home, you are struck immediately by contrast – the simplicity of the interior decoration and the complexity of his artwork. The room itself seems to link the masculine and the feminine: the strong, uncompromising view of the ocean through the picture window which stretches almost the entire width of the living space at one end, and the gentle presence of the soft, mossy, watery, Japanese garden through the French windows at the other.

Almost halfway between the two windows stands Paul's *chakra* altar, which he has not quite completed. He dreamed of this altar as a body with doors which, when opened, would reveal seven shelves. Each shelf or level represents one of the seven chakras and contains objects corresponding to its different aspects. For example, there is a small, clear crystal ball which throws out myriad tiny shafts of light to represent the sixth chakra level – the third eye, the level of clear mind, of illumination; while candles representing primal light stand together with an ostrich egg to represent the connection with earth on the ground, the first level.

Paul tries hard not to let the altar overflow, but it always fills up again because visitors like to bring something and place it in what they feel is an appropriate chakra level. Some day Paul intends to create a rainbow at the top to represent the crown chakra and enlightenment – he just has to work out how. The altar doors are not yet completed, but one day, when he has the energy (for he is both an artist and a writer) Paul will set about fulfilling his dream.

TRAVELLING ALTARS

Kathy Jones and Paul Heussenstamm

Kathy Jones and Paul Heussenstamm feel that if you have
a sacred space, it is not just a belief or a principle, it is spirit
in action. Consequently, they both like to take small
travelling altars with them wherever they go.

Paul says It is important to feel, when you are journeying,
that you have a sacred space to return to, even in a strange
hotel room. He always takes sage, which he burns to clear
any stagnant energy, a candle and one or two pictures that
are meaningful to him.

Kathy likes to take a small altar containing miniatures of the goddess when she is away from home
or, if that is too cumbersome, a small bag of goddess images. Her travelling altar is an eclectic mix
of goddesses, their totem creatures and items from nature that inspire her. Both she and Paul place
statues or pictures on their small altars according to their inner dictates. They may feel that one
image should have more prominence than another or that all should have equal weight. But what
is significant is that they keep their connection to the divine open wherever they might be.

Making your own travelling altar is simple. For many years, Gurmukh and Lori Reid both used old
shoe boxes or small velvet bags, if space was an issue. They emphasise that the beauty of a
travelling altar is that they are always different: what you decide to take with you depends on your
needs and focus at that time. There is always one constant – a god or goddess with which you feel
a special affinity, or some incense, or a shell, or a crystal or a piece of driftwood.

A SHRINE FOR ALL THE FAMILY
NEW JERSEY, USA
Patricia Hess

Like Paul Heussenstamm, Patricia Hess imagined her principal shrine into existence. One night she dreamed that she was looking for a perfect space in which to meditate, and found a tiny temple on a hill covered with Hindu decorations. She felt completely at home in this dream space, even though she had never previously been drawn to Hinduism. But when she later spent some time at Shree Maa's *ashram*, the Devi Mandir, she found a spot there almost identical to the one in her dream. She has followed Shree Maa, known in India as 'the Divine Mother', and Swami Satyananda Saraswati, Shree Maa's greatest devotee, since the time they were invited to bless the Hess's new farm.

It was when Shree Maa and Swami visited the family with twenty of Shree Maa's disciples, that they built the shrine in the living room in gratitude for Patricia's and her husband Charlie's hospitality. 'With this shrine,' said Shree Maa, 'you are bringing God out of the closet.'

Patricia believes that the shrine is transforming her whole family. Shree Maa and Swami taught her son, Justin, to 'smile each day at the coconut' deity they made for the altar because it would make God much more present in his life. Even her daughter, now at an age when she views her mother's spiritual beliefs with deep suspicion, was deeply affected by Shree Maa's presence in the house.

The altar itself is garlanded with daisies and backed with red cloth, and contains images of Ganesh, Vishnu, Buddha, Sekhmet, the Madonna and Jesus, a pot containing sacred water from the Ganges, portraits of the family members and treasured objects, such as a conch shell which they blow on. Patricia always has flowers on the shrine as an offering to each of the deities and to honour the members of her and Charlie's immediate family whose images are there.

Patricia likes to set aside about two hours to perform *puja* (a form of Hindu worship) in the morning before the house is awake and then meditates in the evening, usually in her other space, when the house has gone to sleep.

Patricia's other, smaller shrine-room is more intimate and when she wants to be alone, she comes here. This room reflects not only the shamanistic aspect of her life but also her root to all religions. Again, this altar has Ganesh and Durga in the centre, together with Kuan Yin and Nagakanya, a goddess who manifests herself in all three worlds. Patricia revisits this altar frequently, adding natural objects such as stones or feathers or images according to her needs. She lights candles and incense and makes offerings to the gods as she recites her mantras and she always rings the bell.

Patricia is a professional cellist and has found recently that whilst she is thankful for her classical training, meditation has inspired her to improvise much more freely. 'When I have no printed score to refer to, my music is more of a gift, more of an offering to the Divine.'

A TRADITIONAL BUDDHIST SHRINE ROOM
NEW YORK, USA
Lama Norlha

The purpose of the traditional Buddhist shrine room is to provide a space where people can come together to practise Buddhist teachings through chanting, meditation and ceremony, for in it are representations of the body, speech and mind of the Buddha himself. Tibetan shrine rooms tend to be vivid – the prevailing colours being red and yellow – and dense with statues, mandalas, candles, prayer flags and offertory bowls.

The Lama Norlha spends a considerable amount of time in the shrine room at the monastery in Wappingers Falls, just outside New York (see pages 10 and 92–3), but he considers his shrine room in New York his principal residence. It was created when he arrived in the United States at the urging of the 16th Karmapa to spread the Tibetan message that peace and happiness can ultimately be achieved through meditation, for meditation frees the mind. As Lama Norlha himself puts it, 'I was born at John F. Kennedy Airport in 1976!'

ABOVE: The artist Hans Hokanson treasured his framed Tibetan Buddha, his slender juggler's pin and the gilded idol at the centre of his Buddhist altar as much for their purity of form as for their sacred content.

WORKSHOP AND SKYLIGHT SHRINES

LONG ISLAND, NEW YORK, USA

Barbara Hokanson

Barbara Hokanson keeps the altar created by her late husband much as he left it before he died in 1995. It sits in the corner of a busy basement studio which used to be his workshop and now contains the fruits of Mrs Hokanson's fashion empire. The altar table is made from a mill-wheel base and a simple, hand-carved poplar panel surface. The table originally stood in the living area but both she and her husband Hans, who was a devout Buddhist, decided that it would make a wonderful altar.

An ancient Chinese Buddha takes centre stage in an eclectic mix of dried leaves, a bronze candlestick, some hand-carved wooden eggs, a piece of glass with a scattering of stones in it, a drumstick and a juggler's pin. At first glance it may seem a strange collection, but for the man who made the altar and placed the items there, it was a source of inspiration and celebration. 'They were the things he liked,' says Barbara Hokanson with affection.

Barbara is not a Buddhist, and neither she nor her children use the altar as Hans did, but the knowledge that it is there and was important to him is a source of comfort to her. Barbara herself goes to a small, skylit space in her attic to experience tranquillity and solitude, but nevertheless she continues to tend to her husband's altar. She occasionally burns incense or adds dried or fresh flowers. 'I dust the altar and sometimes toy with it,' she says. 'When Hans was alive, he was constantly rearranging it. But, otherwise, it's very much the way he left it. This is its last incarnation.'

A SHRINE TO MIRROR THE MIND
NEW YORK, USA
John Giorno

The brocade shrine of the poet John Giorno is a glorious confusion of colour, dense with sculptures, icons and personal objects that hold meaning for him. *Gyaltsen* (multi-coloured Tibetan banners symbolising long life) are wound around cylindrical cores; a pair of *bumpas* (wrought silver chalices used as a means of empowerment in Buddhist meditation) are filled with peacock feathers; jewellery inherited from his family; and a spoon 'borrowed' by John from his mother's kitchen can all be found on his altar.

It is this shrine room that John offers to visiting lamas and monks. Each rearranges the altar according to their own tradition, but it is equipped with all the ritual objects and ceremonial implements they need – from a bell, cymbals and drums to offertory bowls. Nevertheless, John has received many gifts for his altar from some of the lamas who have taught here.

John never intended to create a traditional Tibetan altar, but rather to respond to his own inner dictates. As he so eloquently puts it, 'This shrine is the mirror of my mind. I've furnished it with odd bits to suit myself. My shrine departs – it does its own thing – and that's the point. This is a private house and in it is my private temple.'

This is exactly as it should be. We should never feel, when creating an altar, that we have to include a specific item or that it should, as tradition dictates, face east, toward the rising sun. Ultimately a shrine or altar should embody our own souls; intuition should always guide us.

In the

Details

In the Details

Symbols and Talismans

When creating a sacred space, each of the senses has to be considered: sight, hearing, smell, touch – even, in some cases, taste and intuition. These are not so much details as principles, for the senses are of paramount importance when creating a space, altar or shrine.

SCENT

John Steele has been working with essential oils for years and is particularly interested in the phenomenon of synaesthesia, in which one sense, such as smell, stimulates another. As John puts it, 'A fragrance might stimulate the sensory impression of a colour or sound and will alter your perception. I believe that this cross-sensory inspiration is a prerequisite for deep religious, magical and healing states of consciousness. You find frankincense in a church or temple and incense sticks in a meditation room – you simply don't build a shrine without perfume, because perfume is so ethereal and inspirational. There is clear evidence that fragrance has been used in a sacred sense for centuries, in Ancient Egypt and in shamanism in particular.'

John cites the South American shamans known as *perfumeros* whose specialty is to cure with fragrance. They invariably take *ayahuasca* (which literally means 'vine of the spirits'), a hallucinogenic jungle-vine mixture which enables them to see and smell the cause of an illness. 'Each shaman has a slightly different way of enhanced sensing that we would call extrasensory. Sometimes shamans see symbols of the magical origin of an illness. Sometimes they hear magical *icaros* (healing songs). Sometimes, when they smell that a person is out of balance, they give them an aromatic bath and then rub them with fragrant oils. The shaman's breath also has healing power, so often they put perfume in their mouths and, after inhaling tobacco smoke, spray it over their patient. In Spanish this is called *florecer*, which means "to blossom, to make whole."'

John goes on to say that the Mestizos believe shamans cannot heal properly without perfume. Each shaman has an altar containing both Christian and native power objects which are purified and energised before a healing ceremony begins. The Mestizo shamans believe that fragrance is the essential link holding all these power objects together for healing. 'In recent years, we have created a huge divide between mind-spirit and matter. Shamans naturally reintegrate mind and fragrance, and with aromachology and psychoaromatherapy, on a fundamental level, we are attempting to do the same.'

John has been working recently with the company Alaskan Flower Essences to develop a number of sprays which will instantly create sacred space in a room.

Lori Reid agrees wholeheartedly with John Steele· 'Our senses are important because that is how we make a connection. And there must be a connection. Touch and scent are so important around a shrine. Light a candle, burn some incense, use fragrances that remind you of a particular person or that throw up a childhood memory. Nothing is out of place in your sacred space if it touches a chord with you.'

LEFT: Incense has been used through the centuries to heal, to uplift, to inspire and to invoke the sacred.

LEFT: Miranda Holden's meditation room
is painted purple, a colour of Spirit.
RIGHT: Candles can simply decorate or light a
room, but they can also illuminate and inspire.

LIGHT AND COLOUR

Colour and light are often introduced into sacred space. Light may take the form of a candle to represent the eternal flame, or its opposite – lack of light – may be represented by a dark, secluded room. Light in any form can provide a focus for meditation. Colour may be symbolised by the glowing silk cloth on which a statue sits, or its opposite – absence of colour – represented by the pure simplicity of white.

We hardly think about light, unless marvelling at a perfect rainbow, and yet it surrounds us. White light can be made from just three colours, red, green and blue – the primary colours of light; and sunlight is said to be made up of seven colours – red, orange, yellow, green, blue, indigo and violet. But if we consider that the human eye can distinguish any number of different shades of blue, then it is not inconceivable that our eyes can perceive more than 4 billion different colours.

The interfaith minister Miranda Holden has painted her meditation room purple, a colour she loves to wear. 'I made the room beautiful to me because I see beauty as an attribute of Spirit. My husband and I meditate in the room at least once a day. Knowing that the room is there is an invitation to be mindful. Just walking past the room reminds me to stop, take a deep breath and remember what is real, remember my intention, and remember God.'

Miranda holds spiritual healing sessions here and finds that the beauty of the room and its colours always opens up her clients and helps them to communicate. 'My job is to see my clients as they truly are. I hold the vision that in truth they are already whole, and I try to find spiritual frames of reference where they can realize this. Once that happens, clarity on the practical ways forward unfolds. If something traumatic emerges, we go through a healing process together, enabling the client to return to their centre and surrender to the highest truth. We always finish with a meditation.'

For Buddhists, colour is highly symbolic; the pervasive red of a Tibetan Buddhist shrine represents Buddha's speech and conveys compassion. The Ancient Greeks and Ancient Egyptians used both colour and music in their temples to induce an atmosphere of spiritual renewal. Countless books have been written on colour as a healing therapy, providing clear evidence that the colours we wear and by which we are surrounded affect us in some way. Most people know that red is energising, blue is soothing, yellow, like the sun, is a happy colour and green is healing. Perhaps not so many are aware that for the Ancient Egyptians green was a sacred colour – as it is for Moslems today – but that the early Christians banned its use because it was identified with pagan ceremonies celebrating the Green Man, god of fertility.

But regardless of our culture or creed, if we identify those colours that appeal to us most and include them somewhere in our home or meditation space, the colours will resonate with our energy.

SYMBOLS
The Buddha

Sometimes our situation impels us to re-evaluate not just our past, our present and our future, but also prompts us to look at the familiar from a new perspective. Eight years ago the sculptor Arlene

Shechet was facing a life-threatening illness in her family, coping with the death of a close friend and at the same time nearing term in her pregnancy. Life and death seemed to encompass her world, defining her creative impulse. 'If you are an artist, any big experience like this involves a re-examination of what you are doing. Although the twists and turns that you make in life may lead you to this point, a crisis shakes you into action.'

She felt the urge to break away from her previous classical, formal way of working, which required a great deal of preparatory work and planning; she needed to work in an immediate way that focused her completely on the moment. 'When I am sculpting, I find that there are moments of meditative consciousness close to the Buddhist experience. Working with a medium that requires immediate action requires you to suspend conscious planning and enter a state of not thinking – just doing.'

Arlene started to work with plaster, a medium that fascinates her on two counts: it is a powder that becomes a liquid which dries over a short period of time to become a solid; also, working without the classic armature, every second counts because it sets very quickly, requiring complete focus and attention. One day Arlene made a form that she recognised as a Buddha. She realised that working within a spiritual vocabulary, using an iconic form such as the Buddha or the stupa (the architectural version of the Buddha body) perfectly encapsulated what she was attempting to say and do. Feeling the need to add colour, she discovered that if she painted on glass and then removed the 'skin of paint', adding it to the plaster as she wrestled with the form, she was able to use a full range of intense colours and patterns to complement the forms she was making. Colour and form became one. 'The pieces have this feeling of capturing time, of freezing time. The process of creation is inherent in them, it is part of the image, and that is what excites and drives me.'

The Mandala

The mandala is perhaps the most potent symbol of spirituality. A diagrammatic representation of the wholeness of the self and the cosmic order, it usually comprises both a circle and a square divided into four segments or multiples of four. In the Tibetan Buddhist tradition the mandala is regarded as the blueprint for the multidimensional existence of the enlightened state. It can be drawn two-dimensionally on paper or on cloth, created from sand or constructed as a three-dimensional architectural model.

OPPOSITE AND RIGHT: The Buddha and the mandala are two of the most potent manifestations of spirituality found in a sacred space, focusing the mind on the wholeness of the Self and the cosmic order.

The psychologist Carl Jung, like the Tibetans, recognised the mandala as an archetype, an innate concept that is understood universally regardless of race, creed or culture. Both he and the mythologist Joseph Campbell urged that everyone should make their own mandala in order to construct and order their lives – indeed, Jung himself regularly painted a mandala. Because the mandala represents the universal spirit, it is perhaps the most potent symbol on which to meditate; certainly, Jung urged that having first painted a mandala, a meditator should then use it as a powerful tool for meditation, visualisation and transformation.

Paul Heussenstamm finds that painting a personal mandala for a client may take months. But if he waits for the right moment, then the imagery comes to him, his brush flows, and, as he puts it, 'The soul of my client manifests into matter.' Paul is currently writing a book on the spiritual path of art. 'Both Chagall and Gauguin talk a great deal about spirituality in their art and the fact that their hands were guided by something greater than themselves, and Matisse, when asked whether he believed in God, is quoted as saying, "Only when I'm painting!"'

SHAPE

Shirley Wallis, who is a dowser, says shape is critical when creating sacred space. She urges her students to cut out a shape and stand on it, noticing how it alters their perception of space, or to take a compass and draw concentric circles around their homes to see how their world is shaped. Extraordinary energy patterns emerge from this exercise and unseen connections are made. If our ancient ancestors recognised these energy patterns, and learned how to utilize them, so can we. As Shirley says, 'In order to make even the smallest space reflect something back to us, we must bring thought back into the creation of sacred space. We must be the doer, the doing and the deed.'

The circle is a universal symbol representing totality, wholeness, original perfection, unity, enlightenment, God. It is timeless for it has no beginning or end and it is spaceless for it has nothing above or beneath it. In every tradition it is associated with the heavens. A circle with a point at its centre symbolises the sun in astrology and the Tao, the supreme power in Taoism. In Buddhism the circle is the round of existence, in Islam it symbolises divine light, and in Hinduism it represents the round of existence. For the Ancient Greeks the circle symbolised both Time and Fate; for Christians, three interlocking circles depict the Trinity.

The square symbolises the static, fixed nature of the earth as opposed to the dynamic circle of the sky. Squaring the circle brings heaven down to earth in the form of a sacred building, temple or church. The square represents limitation and form, permanence and stability, and is therefore an ideal shape for gardens, courtyards and sacred architecture. It is one of the most important archetypal Hindu symbols, representing the pattern of order in the Universe.

The triangle symbolizes the threefold nature of the universe – heaven, earth and man; mother, father, child; body, soul and spirit. An upward-pointing triangle represents the sun, the masculine principle, the spiritual world and life, a downward-pointing triangle is lunar, representing the feminine principle and the natural world.

The oval represents the feminine – the female life symbol – and is also the halo that encircles a saint. Perhaps the best-known oval shape is the vesica piscis – also known as the *mandorla* – the almond shape created by two intersecting circles that is the basis of all sacred geometry.

ABOVE: Shape and texture, when considered in creating a sacred space, stimulate not only our senses of sight and touch, but also our memories. We are instinctively drawn to those shapes and materials with which we make a specific spiritual association.

TEXTURE

Texture is important to an altar – wood, water, clay, stone, and mirrors have all been used in different cultures and traditions to embody the Divine.

Wood is often the first choice for an altar or for artefacts, because it is one of the five elements and is regarded as sacred in almost every belief system. In the Hindu and Tibetan traditions it is the material out of which all things were shaped. The ash is the Tree of Wisdom in Norse mythology and the oak is considered to be the most sacred tree of all – but which wood to choose is usually a matter of instinct.

Water is universally associated with the feminine and with birth and renewal. Baptism in countless traditions signifies the death of the old life, rebirth into a state of purity and the immersion of the soul in this world. In Celtic lore, water has magical properties and is the home of supernatural entities, such as the Lady of the Lake in Arthurian legend. For the Taoists, water is the visible expression of the doctrine of *wu-wei* – the strength of weakness, the belief that adaptation, change and perseverance, 'going with the flow', will ultimately wear down the strongest resistance.

In Native American tradition, clay or pottery is regarded as a living entity because it comes from the element of earth and, rising phoenix-like, is transfigured by fire, thus giving it spiritual significance.

Stone and rock represents permanence, stability and unity, so for many cultures it is regarded as a symbol both of protection and spiritual endurance. The *omphalos* (Ancient Greek for 'navel') was a round stone kept at the Temple of Apollo at Delphi. It was believed by the Ancient Greeks to mark the middle point of the earth. The word has now come to mean the cosmic centre, the point of communication between God and man. The Ka'aba, a cubic black stone revered by Moslem pilgrims to Mecca, is regarded as an omphalos. In Hinduism, a conical stone, or lingam, symbolises Shiva as creator. In West African traditions, blue stones contain the power of the sky god.

Mirrors are regarded as magical gateways – in some cultures a mirror, if hung face down in a temple or tomb, is believed to offer an 'axis of light' which allow the soul to ascend. In many traditions, mirrors reflect truth and unmask the soul, so they are often used on altars to symbolise mindfulness. The Taoists believe that the mirror is a key symbol for self-realisation, for it reflects not

RIGHT: We are creatures of habit and often the
items we place on altars are chosen, quite apart
from their spiritual significance, because we like
the shape, texture or smell of them.

only the temporal world, but also man's knowledge of himself. Looking in a mirror, the observer will see his nature and, horrified by the reflection, will be impelled to change – for when evil is recognised, it destroys itself.

The main concern when considering textures is that they should appeal to you, speak to you, inspire you. It doesn't matter what you choose to place on your altar, but do pay attention to the textures you use and try using the natural – a feather, a piece of driftwood, some crystals – and materials such as cottons or silks to make prayer flags or to dress an altar.

CRYSTALS

The modern world would not function without crystals, for they represent vital components in much of our technology, including computers, lasers and cars. But crystals also have a very long tradition in healing; contrary to popular belief, they have been regarded as powerful transformational tools for millennia.

Flint was the first crystalline structure to be used extensively (throughout the Stone Age), followed by jade and obsidian – which has been found in Neolithic burial sites. Historically, the most sacred stone of all is probably red ochre, an iron ore which has been associated in almost every culture with the life force and therefore the divine.

The Australian Aborigines regard all crystals as sacred and fundamental to the initiation rite of any shaman or healer. Similarly, in the Native American tradition, crystals were imbued with spiritual and healing power. However, the longest recorded history of the use of crystals for healing is found in Ayurveda, when physicians prescribe powdered gemstones or gem waters in order to balance the *doshas* (body types).

There is no simple explanation why crystals work so effectively with the human body. It has been argued that because a crystal comprises a single molecule, repeated throughout its structure, it maintains a constant electromagnetic vibration and so, like a tuning fork, can retune the body's energies.

Choosing the right crystal to aid healing is once again a matter of intuition. Many people follow the chakra system, choosing stones that correspond to the colour of the chakra that is out of balance: red stones for the base chakra, orange for the sacral, yellow for the solar plexus, green for the heart, blue for the throat, dark blue for the brow or third eye and purple or clear quartz for the crown.

Amethyst and quartz crystal are the most effective stones for use in a meditation space and therefore the most popular. Amethyst is a stone that works well with the brow and crown chakras. Quartz works on all the chakras but also amplifies the energies of any other crystals near it. Placing these stones on an altar or shrine will endow it with the energetic vibration of the crystal, but they can also be used instead of a lighted candle as a focus for meditation.

SOUND

Every sound that you hear is created by something vibrating in the atmosphere. Sometimes you can actually see the vibration; if you hit a tuning fork or pluck a rubber band, you see it vibrating as it sounds, but if you clap your hands it seems as if nothing moves at all. Yet vibration does occur, because air moves around the source of the vibration, creating sound waves that carry the energy of the sound to your ear.

Sound waves, which are measured in hertz cycles per second, form strings which resonate at different frequencies. The faster an object vibrates, the higher the frequency and therefore the higher the pitch. Human hearing range is limited to frequencies between 15 and 20 thousand hertz, but humans reverberate to frequencies much higher and lower than are detectable by the human ear, due to the harmonics created with each note. A harmonic is a note produced at the same time and in mathematical ratio to the first note, so the first harmonic vibrates twice as fast as the original note, the second harmonic three times as fast ... and so on, ad infinitum.

The Greek mathematician and philosopher Pythagoras believed that sounds played in the correct sequence on a musical instrument could alter behaviour patterns and affect mood swings. His beliefs are endorsed by growing numbers of music therapy associations who work to restore, improve and maintain physical, psychological, mental and spiritual health. At Beth Abraham Hospital in the Bronx, research has revealed that with the help of music therapy, patients suffering from Parkinson's Disease are able to once again to organise and perform some of the movements lost to them due to the disease.

Sound is an extraordinary medium and healer. In our deafening world we often forget that a single pure tone or a chant, if used wisely, can re-energize and re-align us. Sound can open each of our chakras; witness the fact that sound is used to prepare the whirling dervish before he or she starts to dance. The idea behind the Sufi chant, *Ya ha hil Allah*, is to prepare the body for whirling by moving the energy through the chakras, onwards and upwards to the crown chakra. The body is moved in a rhythmic way, which imitates the eventual feeling of whirling. It is a circular movement in all four directions, north, east, south, west. Eventually, each individual feels when the moment is right to start whirling. Traditionally, this is done anti-clockwise. One hand leads, raised to the sky, and the other is lower, representing the earth. The dance of the whirling dervish is possibly the deepest meditation of all, because the brain is only able to process a certain number of frames per second from the evidence of the eyes. Whirling increases the number of frames exponentially, and whilst the eyes are capable of seeing all the frames per second, the mind and consciousness are limited. As a result, the whole thought process shuts down, allowing the whirling dervish to enter closer into union with the divine. Whirling can be done for fifteen minutes or for two hours, depending on the meditator. By whirling through the day and night, Rumi, the famous whirling dervish, achieved enlightenment.

Sound can immediately lighten the atmosphere in
a room and create a sense of calm and peace.
LEFT: Jacquie Burgess' bowl is tuned to the note
of F – the note that opens the heart chakra.

Sound can be heard internally when reciting a mantra. It can produce a trance-like state, as in the drumming and chanting central to shamanic practice, or it can inspire the urge to devotion, as in the muezzin's call to prayer. John Gray, author of *Men are from Mars, Women are from Venus*, once conducted a spontaneous group prayer-meditation session on the Oprah Winfrey television show. He asked the audience to stand up, raise their arms slowly above their heads and welcome the divine into their hearts. Whilst some felt compelled to say that they felt a feeling of expansion and peace, others claimed they felt nothing. But to the observer, the effect of the mantra he gave them to repeat was palpable.

Sound can also be cleansing and uplifting when used in meditation. The Brahma Kumaris, who meditate in a group for support and mutual energy, play music throughout their meditation. I myself either meditate outside, with the sound of nature around me, or in my room, where I use a tuning fork or a singing bowl to sound out a single pure note before settling to meditate.

A REVERBERATING SANCTUARY
COUNTY CARLOW, IRELAND
Jacquie Burgess and Herbie Brennan

The crystal singing-bowl in Jacquie Burgess and Herbie Brennan's meditation room focuses attention on the sacred. The bowl is made from completely pure quartz crystal, crushed and heated to 4000° in a centrifugal mould. It was tested, using digital technology, to establish the note the bowl produces, which is F – the note that opens the heart chakra.

When Herbie and Jacquie meditate alone or in a group, they first light a flame within the bowl, to represent the radiance of sanctuary, the sacred flame burning at the heart of their meditation. The bowl is then sounded, using a baton covered in suede. The tone is exquisite, illuminating, cleansing. It reverberates clearly through the meditation space for a minute or more until the ear can no longer detect the sound. But the space itself still embraces the vibration and hums to the note of F on a very subtle level, opening hearts to the divine.

ARRANGING AN ALTAR

Many people feel the need to rearrange their altars, to touch and tend them, in order to create a dynamic relationship with the divine.

Kathy Jones keeps her altar "alive" by continually recreating it, so engaging with the Goddess in a living relationship. Each goddess represents a different expression of the One and the Many – the Maiden, the Mother, the Crone. As different aspects of the Goddess become more dominant at certain times, Kathy feels it is important to give that aspect prominence. The Goddess gives meaning to Kathy's world, and she is fully open to her. Kathy meditates twice a day and finds that her practice intensifies with time.

She first uses bells to cleanse the space with sound vibrations, then lights incense not only to cleanse but also to please the senses. Finally, she lights a candle to connect to the Spirit. She is currently practising the presence of the Lady of Avalon. This includes movement, dancing, bells, candles, incense and singing and then visualising, sitting focused upon the Lady of Avalon, Goddess of Glastonbury, Goddess of Transformation, Death and Rebirth.

TALISMANS

From time immemorial, people have worn talismans and lucky charms or carried crystals or stones in their pockets to protect and restore. In his book *Bodyguards*, the anthropologist Desmond Morris shares with readers his enduring fascination with the power of the talisman. Over forty years of studying the human species he has found that, regardless of where he travels and whatever the culture, talismans are universal. In some countries they are used to protect from bad luck, in others to bring the bearer good fortune. Regardless of its provenance, the talisman or charm is treated with respect worldwide and endowed with beneficial, divine, even magical properties for it is, in effect, portable sacred space.

In Tibet, the *thogchag* (protective amulet) is shrouded in mystery. It was believed to have fallen, magically-formed, from the sky and was used by healers and shamans in pre-Buddhist rituals. The Ancient Egyptians wore an amulet, taking it to the grave with them. They were buried with two amulets:

the *ded*, a pillar-shaped amulet signifying the backbone of Osiris and their safe passage into the next world, and one dedicated to Isis to grant them rebirth. During the Late Bronze Age scarabs, previously used as royal seals, were used as amulets, decorated with good luck inscriptions, often containing the name of the god Amon-Re. The Romans wore key-shaped amulets to invoke the protection of Janus, the two-faced god who looks back into the past and forward into the future. The amulet not only afforded Janus' protection, but also symbolised the threshold between this world and the next.

ARTEFACTS

We respect and honour the items we place on our altars and in our homes because they are there not just to serve our own needs, but for a specific purpose. They represent those things that give meaning and shape to our lives. They support our beliefs, embody our faith and allow us an experiential relationship with the divine. We may wish to honour the Hindu gods: Shiva the three-faced god who creates, protects and destroys, his son Ganesh, the remover of obstacles, or Lakshmi, consort of Vishnu, goddess of prosperity and good luck. We may choose to honour the Buddha, or Kuan Yin, the Chinese goddess of compassion and mercy, or Bast, the Egyptian goddess of life, or Gaia, the earth itself. We may use the cross, an *ankh* (the Egyptian cross of life) or a *caduceus*, representing the tree of life and adopted by the medical profession as its symbol. Perhaps we pay homage to animal totems, chosen for the characteristics we wish to celebrate, or else we place nature's gifts on our shrine as offerings – water, grain, salt, crystals, flowers or fruit.

GODDESS OF THE KITCHEN
NEW YORK, USA
Alice Harris

For Alice Harris, there is one image in her home that defines the spiritual in her life. The instant you step through the door into her cherry-wood kitchen, you are struck by its warmth and by the gentle, soft energy that pervades the room. Rounding the corner of a kitchen cabinet you see for the first time the deity on the end wall which presides over the room with a nurturing calm and benevolence. This marvellous piece came from a Japanese temple and dates back to the 17th century. Alice confesses that the minute she saw her kitchen goddess she had to contain her excitement, because she knew instinctively that this deity would protect her family and that she somehow had to acquire her.

Alice's first wish for her family is for them to enjoy good health and good fortune, and this is what the goddess provides. 'She watches over my family at every meal and she exudes a wonderful peace and joy. This is our favourite room because of her. I'd like to believe that she is part earth-mother, part woman of abundance – but whoever she really is, she is a great deity. Because she looks after us, I look after her. I dust her regularly, polish her gently and shield her from the midday sun, and I always have fresh flowers – orchids – surrounding her. In the early evening a halo of light arches in from the west through the window and it is almost as if she comes alive.'

PRAYER AND MEDITATION

Prayer need not be confined to any one space, even though we often choose a particular area that resonates with our souls. When we create sacred space in our own environment, there are no rules, only instinct. Some people carry their sacred space with them, either in the work they do for others, or in the form of a travelling altar. For others, the urge to meditate can be met anywhere. Paul Wilson, author of *The Little Book of Calm*, says that a couple of years ago, he built a studio with a pyramid ceiling. It was intended to be a yoga and meditation space. 'The trouble is, I've never really got around to using it for that purpose. It has been a recording studio and work station – everything but a meditation space. The truth is that I can meditate wherever it's quiet and I have a little space. In the past eighteen months, I've discovered surfing, and spend endless hours out on the back of the waves, sitting on the board, relishing the peace. Quirky, perhaps, as a meditation spot, but wonderful!'

RIGHT: The Buddha on Frances Heussenstamm's altar is flanked by countless pieces from every faith tradition to celebrate spiritual diversity

AN EVER-CHANGING ALTAR
CALIFORNIA, USA
Frances Heussenstamm

Frances Heussenstamm is a psychotherapist by profession and a spiritual artist by inspiration. She paints life in the cycle of birth and rebirth. For her, all world religions, faiths, beliefs, hold something sacred and meaningful and should be celebrated. 'There is room in my consciousness for everyone and for whatever belief they hold that comforts and supports them. I have long since surrendered to a force larger than we are, and that force is breathing me. I wake up grateful for every breath secure in that knowledge.'

Her altar contains, amongst other things, soil from Africa; a copy of the *Torah*; the eye of Horus (because the Jews believe that they carry the energy of Egypt in an unbroken line), Shiva; ashes to represent Zoroaster; a Native American wedding vessel to symbolise the union of the earth and the stars; the Buddha flanked by images of the dark and light feminine principle represented by Kuan Yin (Avalokiteshvara or Kannon); a Chinese funerary sculpture to remind Frances of the *Tao*, the teachings of Confucius and reverence for her ancestors; text from the *Qu'ran*, and a stone from Bali to hold incense.

Frances' altar is an ever-changing, evolving sacred space, as she finds small pieces that speak to her of faith and truth beyond the material world. 'My altar and I represent a bridge between the old age and the new, between long-held beliefs and faiths and a new, burgeoning, non-denominational spirituality.'

It is with Frances' altar that I have chosen to close this book, because her shrine reflects an essential truth: the path to understanding and peace is found through enlightenment. What hope is there for humanity if we cannot learn to celebrate our differences? As His Holiness the Dalai Lama says, whilst religion is something that we may well be able to do without, the spiritual qualities of love and compassion are fundamental to existence.

Glossary

Amulet: Charm worn or carried to protect against witchcraft, ill-fortune or accident.

Aromachology: Science researching the effect of scent on behaviour and mood.

Artha: The great she-bear who reigns in the heavens.

Ashram: Hindu retreat that fosters spiritual growth in the life of a Hindu. There are four accepted ashrams or stages of life: Bramacharya (studying), Grihastha (domestic, as a married man and breadwinner), Vanaprastha (performing penance) and Sanyasa (renouncing worldly attachments).

Avalokiteshvara [Also known as **Kannon** or **Kuan Yin**]: The bodhisattva of compassion. Traditionally Tibet is the land of this bodhisattva, the Tibetan people are his descendants, and the Dalai Lamas are his human manifestations.

Ayahuasca: Vine-like Brazilian plant with powerful hallucinogenic effects.

Ayurveda: Ancient Hindu text on the art of healing and prolonging life.

Black Tara: Feminine aspect of the bodhisattva of compassion, known as 'Mother of all the Buddhas'.

Bodhicitta: In Tibetan Buddhism, the embodiment of compassion; the attitude of cherishing all things above the self.

Bodhisattva: Individual motivated by bodhicitta – compassion – to seek enlightenment for themselves and for others.

Brahma Kumaris: The Brahma Kumaris World Spiritual University teaches meditation as a means of rediscovering inner strength. Its founder Brahma Baba recognized kindness, patience, tolerance, sacrifice and love as core values in the process of global spiritual transformation. In October 1937 he surrendered all his assets to a management committee run by eight young women. The organization continues to be largely administered by women, fostering harmony between the sexes and partnerships rooted in spirituality.

Brigit: Celtic triple fire goddess (the fire of inspiration, the fire of healing and the fire itself); the cow goddess and the sun goddess, often known as the White Swan.

Buddha, Shakyamuni: Title given to Sidharta Gautama, the Buddha, or Enlightened One.

Buddhism: Faith founded in Northern India by Siddharta Gautama (563–483 BCE), who later took the name Buddha. It teaches that each of us has an embryo of enlightenment within us and that, if properly nurtured, it will allow us to become enlightened, ideal people, with supreme knowledge, love and compassion. It is attained by first understanding the Four Noble Truths – *dukkha* (suffering which must be understood in order to become enlightened) *samudaya* (the greed that causes dukkha), *nirodha* (the cure for dukkha, overcoming selfishness and craving) and *magga* (the middle way of the Eightfold Path, developing moral and mental capacity to raise us from the worldly to the spiritual). The Buddha's Eightfold Path shows how to attain enlightenment by following the path of right belief, resolution, speech, action, living, effort, mindfulness and peace of mind through meditation.

Buddhism, Mahayana: Form of Northern Buddhism mainly found in China, Japan, Tibet and Korea, which splintered from the Theravadan Buddhist tradition. Mahayana Buddhists believe that they should help others find nirvana rather than seeking it for themselves.

Buddhism, Theravadan: Also known as Forest Buddhism or Southern Buddhism, and originating in Burma, Sri Lanka and Thailand, it teaches that since Buddha was a human being who reached nirvana entirely through his own efforts, each of us must journey across the sea of life alone to seek nirvana for ourselves.

Buddhism, Tibetan: Buddhism became Tibet's state religion in 173 CE but splintered into five principal spiritual traditions; Bön (the oldest tradition), Nyingma, Sakya, Kagyu, and Kadampa, which inspired the development of the Gelug tradition. Tibetan Buddhist practitioners wish to end not only their own suffering but also the suffering of all sentient beings, to whom they owe a karmic debt. Tibetan Buddhists work to develop the mindfulness that arises out of meditation.

Buddhism, Zen: 'Zen' is a Japanese translation of the Sanskrit word *Dhyana*, meaning 'meditation'. Zen Buddhists come from the Mahayana Buddhist tradition and follow the example of the Buddha in his quest for enlightenment. Whilst some schools of Buddhism stress the importance of chanting and elaborate symbolism, Zen promotes meditation as a way of finding enlightenment.

Celtic Calendar: According to the ancient Celtic Calendar, north represents the Winter Solstice, south, the Summer Solstice, east the Spring Equinox and west the Autumn Equinox. The eastern quarter is the place of air, the rising sun, spring, re-generation and promise; the south is the quarter of fire associated with summer, light, heat, passion and growth. The west is the quarter of water, the setting sun, autumn, fruitfulness, maturity and the moon and tides; while the north represents earth, winter, night, cold, wisdom and might. The four secondary directions represent the four festivals of the Celtic year. Imbolc, in the north-east, is associated with the goddess Brighid, or Brigit, birth, childhood and the growth energy of Spring. Beltane, in the south-east, marks the start of summer when the entrance to the Otherworld is said to be flung open. It is a time of ardour, beauty and vitality and the May Queen and maypole ceremony are its last vestiges. Lugnasadh (or Lammas) in the south-west is the harvest festival. Named for the god Lugh, it was traditionally the time for electing chieftains and kings and is for assessing the past and evaluating the future. Samain in the north-west marks the start of the Celtic year, a time to sow, honour the past, cleanse and communicate with inner worlds.

Chakra: Spinning vortex of energy within the body.

Chaurasi: Endless cycle of birth and rebirth, also known as *samsara*. (see **Hinduism**)

Chi: Invisible energy field in the environment and in the body, sometimes known as vital force or life force.

Chi Kung: Series of postures and exercises designed to facilitate the free flow of chi through the body to optimise physical stamina and flexibility.

Collective unconscious: Term coined by Carl Gustav Jung to describe the shared pool of cultural memories, knowledge and experience that is accessible to everyone, regardless of race, creed or culture.

Confucius: Chinese philosopher and teacher (551–478 BCE) who founded an ethical system based on worship of and devotion to ancestors, family and friends and the preservation of justice and peace. His teachings emphasised the value of *li* (ritual and etiquette), *hsiao* (love for family and ancestors), *yi* (rectitude), *chung* (loyal patriotism), *xin* (honesty) and *jen* (philanthropy – the greatest Confucian virtue).

Copal: Resin used by the Mayan Indians for purification purposes.

Crystals: Solid form assumed by many minerals, exhibiting definite symmetrical and geometrical planes and facets that reflect the internal atomic structure. Each crystal is composed of a single molecule, repeated endlessly throughout its structure.

Divining rod: Forked twig, often of witch hazel, held by the tips, which bends downward when over a source of hidden water or mineral deposit.

Dowsing: Ancient art of searching for anything hidden, whether water, minerals, ore, oil, missing items, or of diagnosing and treating a person by tapping into the collective unconscious. Dowsers or diviners use a y- or l-shaped divining rod or pendulum, often a crystal or key chain. A skilful dowser can assess earth energies and locate anything from a source of water in an arid climate to an allergy in a patient.

Durga: Hindu mother goddess and female principle that activates Shiva and is the personification of universal energy. Durga is Pavarti in her formidable form. She is a composite goddess, with elements of many gods and goddesses.

Eloheim, Star of: Seven-pointed star, the star of God or the gods.

Enso: Shape drawn when a Zen calligrapher takes up his brush whilst meditating on the blank paper in front of him. At the perfect moment, he paints the circle on the page. This circle holds not only the perfection of that precise creative moment but also the flaws of the ink, the brush and the hand that guides it. The circle can represent a wheel or the full moon, or more profoundly the circle of life, the moment of enlightenment.

Feng Shui: Refined art of Chinese geomancy seeking to enhance luck and well-being by modifying the layout and orientation of homes or work-places, so that individuals may exist in harmony with their natural environment.

Five elements: In the Western tradition, the five elements are air, earth, fire, water and wood. In the Chinese tradition and in Feng Shui they are earth, wood, fire, metal and water. In Ayurveda, the five elements are ether/space, air, fire, water and earth.

Gaia: In Greek mythology, the Earth, worshipped as the mother and nourisher of all things. In the 1970s James Lovelock propounded the 'Gaia hypothesis', suggesting that the Earth is a self-regulating super-organism.

Ganesh: Virtual son of Shiva and his consort Pavarti, depicted with the head of an elephant, a fat human body and four arms; the best beloved of all Hindu gods who removes obstacles, bringing prosperity, wisdom and success.

Glastonbury: Town in Somerset, England renowned for its spiritual associations. Many believe that it is situated at the heart of the legendary Isle of Avalon.

Glastonbury Zodiac: Seen from above, the contours of road and land around the town of Glastonbury are believed by many to take the form of an ancient zodiac. Wearyall Hill represents Pisces and the Tor forms part of a giant phoenix, so the Upper Room, situated between them, links the Piscean age, when Christianity crystallised into one form, and the emerging Aquarian age, in which spirituality is becoming more universal.

Mantra: Sanskrit for 'instrument of thought'; a prayer or phrase which, when chanted repeatedly either out loud or silently in meditation, stills the mind and brings a sense of peace.

Goddess: Female divinity, worshipped as the three in one – Maiden, Mother and Crone.

Guru: Hindu teacher who provides spiritual leadership and knowledge.

Hand fast: Contract sealed by the clasping of hands – traditionally, a betrothal or marriage ceremony

Hanuman: Monkey god of Hindu mythology, associated with loyalty, courage and religious devotion.

Hinduism: Henotheistic religion acknowledging a single deity, Brahman, but also recognising other gods or goddesses as different aspects of the supreme God. The principle of Brahman is that the entire universe is a single divine entity at one with the universe but simultaneously transcending it. Brahman is visualised as a trinity – Brahma the Creator, Vishnu (Krishna) the Preserver, and Shiva the Destroyer. Some Hindus regard Vishnu as the principal deity, others follow Shiva as the ultimate godhead. Hindus believe in reincarnation, the repeated transfer of the soul after death into another body, which in turn leads to *samsara* or *chaurasi* – the continuous cycle of birth, death and rebirth. They also believe that *karma* – the accumulation of a person's good and bad deeds – determines the quality of their next life.

Horus: Falcon-headed god of Ancient Egypt and son of Osiris and Isis, who avenged his father's murder, united Upper and Lower Egypt and became god of order and justice.

Icaro: Healing song often heard by the South American Indian shamans when performing a healing ceremony.

Islam: Religious system established by the prophet Mohammed (Islam means 'peace'). Moslems believe that there is but one God, Allah, and that Mohammed is his prophet; that Islam is a continuation of the faith taught by the Jewish and Christian prophets Noah, Abraham, Isaac, Ismail, Jacob, Moses, David and Jesus; and that Mohammed, born in 570 CE in Mecca, was the last Prophet of God, entrusted with clarifying and purifying the faith. The two sacred texts of Islam are the *Qu'ran*, believed to be the exact word of God given to Mohammed, and the *Hadith*, a collection of Mohammed's sayings (*sunnah*) and an account of his works (*seerah*). Moslems follow the five pillars of Islam: *shahada*, a creed pledging that there is only one god and that Mohammed is his messenger; *salat*, five daily prayers facing Mecca; *saum*, abstaining from food, liquids and marital sexual relations between dawn and sunset during the month of Ramadan (the month when Mohammed received the Qu'ran from Allah); *zakat*, an annual donation of a 2.5% charity tax; and *haj* – every Moslem tries to make a pilgrimage to Mecca once during their lifetime.

Islamic garden: Garden designed on Islamic principles. The *Qu'ran* says there were four rivers in Paradise; one water, one honey, one milk and one wine. The Persians believed that the universe was divided into four squares with the spring of life at its centre. This belief is echoed in the traditional fourfold Islamic garden, designed to incorporate water, a circle symbolising heaven and squares representing order and nature. Usually the garden also contains a *talar*, a porch-like edifice which provides shade and is regarded as the gateway between the spiritual and terrestrial planes, the garden representing spirit, the buildings representing the body.

Japanese Tea Ceremony: Precisely-structured ritual of sharing tea. Host and guests refresh and cleanse themselves at the *tsukubai* (a stone basin) then proceed through the *chumon* (middle gate) or threshold between the manifest world and the spiritual world of tea. The tea-house itself is undecorated, save for a *kakemono* (scroll painting), and sometimes flowers. Deep significance is given to the host's ritual of preparing and serving the tea to his guests.

Jizoo Bosatsu: Protector of children, pregnant women and travellers, traditionally found at crossroads. He was imported to Japan from China and became popular as a bodhisattva, saving common sinners from hell.

Kannon: Another name for Avalokiteshvara, the bodhisattva of compassion.

Kerridwen: Goddess of the underworld; the great white sow, into whose cauldron all souls return for inspiration and regeneration.

Kuan Yin: Chinese Buddhist bodhisattva of compassion and mercy, also identified with Avalokiteshvara, Kannon and Green Tara.

Kundalini: Psychic energy, sometimes known as *shakti*, visualised as a sleeping serpent and found at the base of the spine. When awakened, it climbs up the spinal column to the crown chakra.

Lady of Fatima, Our: Manifestation of the Blessed Virgin Mary believed to have appeared six times to children in the village of Fatima, Portugal in 1917, urging peace on mankind.

Lama: High-ranking Tibetan Buddhist priest or monk.

Ley lines: Electromagnetic force fields penetrating the earth at points known as nodes. Entering the earth, they run to a depth of 265 feet then break at right angles and travel in a straight line for up to thousands of miles, although their average length is between 20-30 feet. To exit the earth, they again make a 90° turn and pass through the centre of the earth, coming out on the other side. A yang energy field extends upward from a ley line through any building that crosses it. If positive, it is thought to cause an energy surge or hyperactivity; if negative, tension or anxiety.

Li: Visible effect of chi – ripples across a lake, or the wind swirling in a field of grain.

Lingam: Conical stone representing the Hindu deity Shiva.

Mala: Tibetan prayer beads.

Mandala: Diagrammatic representation of the wholeness of the self and the cosmic order, comprising a circle and a square divided into four segments or multiples of four. In the Tibetan Buddhist tradition it is regarded as the blueprint for the multidimensional existence of the enlightened state.

Mentorship: Advice and encouragement given by a teacher or guide.

Mesa Verde: Area in south-west Colorado containing the ruins of primitive prehistoric cliff-dwellings and declared an American National Park in 1906.

Mestizos: In Mexico and the western United States, a person of mixed Spanish and Indian blood.

Mexican Day of the Dead: Day on which the Mexicans honour their ancestors and deceased loved ones with feasting and celebration.

Mudra: Sacred ritual gesture of hand. In yoga, symbolic mantras relating to the energy of a particular meditation.

Muezzin: Mosque official who calls the Moslem faithful to prayer.

Native American Medicine Wheel: Wheel symbolizing the circle of life and whole universe. It usually resembles a wagon wheel with a cairn or hub at the centre surrounded by a circle of stones, with a line of stones linking the central cairn and the stones encircling it. The medicine wheel reveals the journey an individual must take to be fully human, and shows the path back home.

Nirvana: Conquest of Self and subsequent freedom from mortality.

Nuristani: Originating from a mountainous district in north-east Afghanistan.

Perfumero: South American shaman who heals using fragrance.

Power centres: Centres created when both ley lines and underground water are found at the source of a ley line. Power centres represent a fusion of yin and yang and therefore a balanced holistic field which is greater than that of a ley or water line. They are believed not only to transform human consciousness but also to retain some of the energy and emotion of anyone who has visited that particular sacred site or monument.

Puja: Formalised Hindu worship using an image that represents a deity to focus the senses on the Divine through invocations, prayers, songs and rituals.

Reflecting pool: Shallow pool of water used for meditation or reflection.

Roji: Japanese Tea garden or *roji-niwa* (*roji* means 'dew path'). It is divided into two gardens. The outer garden (*soto-roji*) contains a waiting station (*machiai*) for the tea ceremony. The inner garden (*uchi-roji*) is accessed via a *chumon* – a small gate separating the spiritual garden immediately surrounding the tea-house from the manifest world beyond.

Rumi, Jalaluddin Mevlana: Persian poet and mystic of the Sufi tradition, he founded the Mevlevi Order, also known as Whirling Dervishes, in the 13th century, using dance as a way to achieve oneness with God.

Sanyasin: Man or woman (*sanyasini*) who renounces all worldly attachments and follows the path of *dharma*.

Scarab: Gem or stone inscribed with symbols and carved in the shape of a large, black dung beetle, used as an amulet by the Ancient Egyptians to represent fertility and resurrection.

Sekhmet: Egyptian sun goddess and goddess of war, usually depicted as a woman with the head of a lioness.

Shaman: Tribal medicine man, wizard or magician associated with the North, Middle and South American Indian traditions.

Shiva: Hindu god of destruction and reproduction.

Sikhism: Monotheistic religion founded by Guru Nanak (1469–1538) combining the teachings of Persian Sufism with Hinduism. It does not believe that God takes a human form (*Avtarvada*) nor does it attach any importance to gods, goddesses or other deities. Elevating the Sikh Scripture (Sri Guru Granth Sahib) to the status of the everlasting guru, it promotes *bhakti marg* (the path of devotion), *gian marg* (the path of knowledge) and *karam marg* (the path of action). Humanity's goal is to merge with God by following the teachings of the guru, meditating and performing acts of charity.

Source: God, the Creator, from whence we come and whence we will return.

Spider Woman: Earth goddess in Hopi Indian legend, who created creatures, birds, plants, men and women out of clay.. She sits at the centre of the galaxy and draws people together in her web.

Spiral: Since it moves into the centre and out again in a constant flow, a spiral is believed by many to hold much of the energy of the number nine. It is a feminine instinctive energy which can depict waxing and waning and also birth and death.

Stone circle: Stone circles are found in Europe, the Middle East, Africa, North America and Canada and are believed to mark the ley lines, water lines and power centres on which they stand. Each stone denotes an astronomical alignment such as True North, the Solstices, May Day, Lammas and the Equinoxes.

Stupa: Buddhist shrine, dome or tower containing Buddhist relics or indicating the presence of the sacred.

Sufism: Moslem system of philosophical and devotional mysticism which has inspired religious poetry and is particularly associated with Persia.

Synaesthesia: Phenomenon in which one sense, such as smell, stimulates another.

Taoism: Religious system founded in China by Lao-Tzu, a contemporary of Confucius. The *Tao-te-Ching*, a set of writings intended to help end feudal warfare, describes the nature of life, the way to peace and how a leader should conduct his life. The ultimate goal of Taoism is to become one with the *Tao* (path), a force flowing through everything Taoists believe in the ultimate goodness of human nature and the philosophy of 'do as you would be done by'. Taoism became a state religion in 440 CE.

Thangka: Elaborate depiction of the Buddha's various forms and teachings.

Third Eye: Chakra centre, also known as the brow chakra, situated on the forehead between and just above the level of the eyes.

Torah: Hebrew for 'law' or 'doctrine', the *Torah* represents the entire Judaic scriptures – the oral Torah and the *Pentateuch* or written *Torah* – together with commentaries on them.

Triple Goddess: Concept of the Great Goddess as young woman (Maiden), birth-giving matron (Mother) and old woman (Crone), dating from the earliest ages of humankind. These attributes were also ascribed to the three phases of the moon – new, full and waning.

Vedas: Sacred literature of Hinduism, the *Vedas* were originally transmitted orally and transcribed into Sanskrit around the 3rd Century BCE. The four *Vedas*, the *Rig-Veda*, the *Sama-Veda*, the *Yajur-Veda* and the *Atharva-Veda* are collectively referred to as the *Samhitas*.

Vesica piscis: Design representing the proportions to which all English cathedrals were constructed, and linked to ancient sites, to the Pythagorean harmonics in the elemental table and to the movement of the planets and the stars. Two circles joined together represent spirit and matter, *yin and yang*, light and dark, masculine and feminine and the interdependence of the two.

Water lines: Underground streams undulating beneath the Earth's surface and creating a vertical electromagnetic field several feet wide, which is *yin* in energy and thought to be enervating.

Whirling dervish: Dervishes, known as the Mevlevi Order, from the Sufi offshoot of Islam. They perform a prayer trance ritual whilst whirling around their own axis. As they dance, they raise their right hand, palm up, so that energy enters from above, passing through their body and their left palm – which faces down to the earth.

Yang: A complementary opposite in Chinese philosophy. *Yang* cannot exist without *yin*, for one gives the other meaning. *Yang* is the masculine principle; the sun, light, movement, noise, and life.

Yin: A complementary opposite in Chinese philosophy. *Yin* cannot exist without *yang*, for each contains a kernel of the other. *Yin* is the feminine principle; the moon, darkness, stillness, silence, and death.

Yoga, Iyengar: Form of yoga developed by B.K.S. Iyengar in the mid-20th century promoting flexibility, balance and strength through breathing and precise poses (*asanas*). It is highly regarded as a remedial yoga because of its slow precise movements, attention to detail and use of props.

Yoga, Kundalini: A sequence of yoga exercises including *pranayama* (breathing exercises), *bhandas* (body locks), and *kriyas* (exercise sets), using *asanas* (postures), *mudras* (hand gestures) and *mantras* (repeated chanted words). Kundalini yoga awakens the kundalini energy up the spine to the crown chakra, inducing a transcendental spiritual state. Believed to be over 50,000 years old, it was brought to the west by Yogi Bhajan.

Zen do: Buddhist meditation hall.

Zoroastrianism: Religious system founded by Zarathustra (Zoroaster) in Persia around 1500–1000 BCE asserting that there is a single, supreme god, *Ahura Mazda*. Its followers are dedicated to a simple creed – good thoughts, good words, good deeds. It is believed that human beings communicate with god through *amesha spentas* ('bounteous immortals'). Within the *Avesta* – the Zoroastrian holy book containing the original words of Zarathustra – these immortals are sometimes conceptual, sometimes personified. The *Gathas* endorse the worship of one god, encourage an understanding of cosmic order and emphasise individual choice in ethical behaviour.

Index

Acknowledgments

I give thanks that I have had the good fortune to write this book. It seems that every time I opened a door and met one person, four more doors opened and I encountered countless other inspirational places and people. They have given me their wisdom and insight and opened their hearts in the most extraordinary fashion. Being prepared to share these, their most intimate of spaces, with others, is no small undertaking and speaks eloquently of their generosity.

Sadly, I could not include the work of Eva Jiricna, architect of the Faith Section of the Millennium Dome in London, now dismantled. The central chamber, a canvas cupola lit subtly with pink and blue light, was intended by Jiricna to be quiet, still and non-denominational. She succeeded: the calm of this room appealed to everyone who set foot in it and belied the frenetic activity outside.

There are many places and people I did not meet on my journeying. I regret that I never met Blake Foster, known as Blake the Angel. Diagnosed with cancer, she turned further and further to spirituality to give meaning to her own and others' lives. She can be seen on the streets of New York City, dressed as an angel, dispensing blessings to those that need them. She carries her sacred space within her, sharing it with others. I also regret that we did not photograph the work of Sara Allan, a shepherdess-turned-inspirational painter who is the medium for the guardian spirit Emmanuel; nor could I cover Miriam's Well, a healing garden in the Caitskills outside New York; nor the Roth Center in East Hampton, Long Island, where spirituality is taught as part of the curriculum; nor Sting's meditation space in Wiltshire; nor the Prince of Wales's Islamic garden.

I would like to gratefully acknowledge the immeasurable contributions made to this book by the following people: Sarah Allan, Ken and Ann Allen, Philip Anthony, the Avalon Foundation, Amarjeet Bhamra, Barbara Biziou, Anthony Bovill, Jacquie Burgess and Herbie Brennan, the Chalice Well Trust, Clodagh, Barbara Corcoran, Alison and Anthony Crichton-Stuart, Jill Davies, Scott Durkin, Allison Fonte, Elise Frick, Uri Geller, Julia Gibson, Michelle Gibson, Father John Gilligan, John Giorno, Tara Guber, Gurmukh, Alice Harris, Patricia Hess, Frances and Paul Heussenstamm, Barbara Hokanson, Miranda Holden, Eva Jiricna, Julia and Virginia Johnson, Kathy Jones, David and Ginny Kidd, Joan and Graeme Kidd, Raymond and Deneen King, Hedi Kleinman, Ruth La Ferla, Isis Livingstone, Southerlyn Marino, Peter Mathiessen, Nitya, Argon Nixon, Lama Norlha, Miriam Novalle, Stephen Pearce, Lori Reid, Carol and Chris Rudd, Gez Sagar, Richard St Ruth, Wendy Sarasohn, Danny Seo, Pierre Sernet, Pamela Serrure, Arlene Shechet, Kimberley Sheppey, Sister Briegeen and the Sisters of St Clare, Eric Small, Ben Southwell, John Steele, Kenneth Thompson, Diane Von Furstenberg, Shirley Wallis, Paul Wilson, Jackie and Michael Young.